CHARLTON'S CHAMPIONS

Charlton's Champions

Gordon Cox

Edited by

Eric Paylor

Original Concept and Production

John Wilson

First published in Great Britain by
Juniper Publishing, Juniper House,
3, Sandy Lane, Melling, Liverpool, L31 1EJ
1999

ISBN 09528622 3 9

Typesetting and origination by:
P's and Q's Ltd., Unit 10, Gibraltar Row,
King Edward Industrial Estate, Liverpool L3 7HJ

Printed and bound by:
Albion Graphics, Old Connelly Complex,
Kirkby Bank Road, Knowsley Industrial
Park North, Kirkby Merseyside L33 7SY

CONTENTS

*This book is dedicated to the memory of my late father Don,
who first introduced me to the game in 1967 when I was 7.*

ACKNOWLEDGEMENTS

Grateful thanks to all who contributed in more ways than one.

To Lauri, Jamie, Sarah and my mother Anne, all of whom have seen little of me over the last few months. That may be a good thing!

To Dave Thomas, Martin Stockton, Ken Daly, Eric Paylor and Alastair Brownlee, all trusted friends.

To the staff of Middlesbrough and Stockton-on-Tees reference libraries and John Wilson for their considerable professional help.

In addition I would like to thank the Middlesbrough Evening Gazette for their commitment to this project, particularly with regard to the supply of photographs and to the Middlesbrough FC Memorabilia Society for vital background information.

CHAPTER ONE
BEGINNINGS

STAN Anderson announced his shock resignation as manager in January, 1973, leaving Middlesbrough Football Club at the crossroads.

Anderson, an immensely talented former playing captain of Newcastle United, Sunderland and the Boro, had been an effective and committed manager on Teesside during almost seven years at the helm. He had brought tremendous stability to the club after winning promotion at the first attempt to take the club out of the Third Division.

Unfortunately Stan's bold and concerted attempts to take Boro back to the First Division were destined to end in failure, despite several near misses. In five completed seasons in this division under his reign, Boro finished sixth, fourth, fourth, seventh and ninth. Season after season of great anticipation had ended in disappointment for manager, players and fans alike.

The board of directors at Ayresome Park continued to back Anderson to the hilt. In November, 1972, he was offered a new three-year contract. The deal was worth an impressive £6,500 a year and was back-dated until July. The directors continued to believe that Stan was the man to take the club forward and had backed their judgement by offering him this tempting new contract. But Anderson was a man of principle. More than most, he was becoming increasingly frustrated by the succession of seasons which promised so much but ended with only embitterment, as other clubs were promoted instead. So Anderson, believing that the 1972-73 season was make or break for himself and his team, went back to the board and requested a one-year contract.

This unselfish move left no doubts that Anderson had the club's best interests at heart. Results had not been up to scratch in the early part of the 1972-73 season and he was not certain whether he could take the Teessiders any further forward. Boro had put together a promising unbeaten run of eight games in September and early October, but performances had slipped again.

Stan also wondered whether he was getting the best out of one or two players, after having been at the helm at Ayresome Park since April, 1966. Perhaps familiarity was creeping in and it was time to move on to pastures new.

Anderson's reign finally came to an end two months after he had been offered the new deal. He announced

Stan Anderson who, without question, left Jack Charlton a squad of great potential.

publicly on January 25 that he was resigning. He made his brave decision less than a fortnight following a disappointing Boro display in a 1-0 defeat at Plymouth Argyle in the third round of the FA Cup.

The Boro directors, shocked by Anderson's decision, pleaded with him to change his mind. But Anderson was adamant. He left the club immediately and bade an emotional farewell to the first team squad, many of whom, like striker John Hickton, had played under his wing for several years.

There was mixed reaction from the fans, though many felt that the time had come for a new face in the manager's chair. Like the manager, they had become frustrated by the continual failure of the club to make the final leap into the First Division. But there was no animosity. Stan left with the supporters' best wishes. He was a respected manager. He left the club with his head held high. He had put together a good quality squad which contained a strong blend of youth and experience. All it needed was the spark to ignite the fuse.

In this respect, Boro were at the crossroads when Anderson cleared his desk for the final time. The machinery was in place, because there were plenty of ace cards in the dressing room. There was also ambition in the board room. But the club would not go forward unless the right replacement was found for Stan Anderson. Suddenly, there was a lot of pressure on the board to ensure that the right man was appointed.

Were the directors prepared to row the boat out and bring in a big name manager who would be guaranteed to bring an immediate response from both players and fans? Or would they gamble with a lesser name, who might not have the talents to inspire the Boro squad to greater things in the short term?

It was a big decision facing the board. No new manager had been appointed at Ayresome Park since 1966, when Anderson stepped into the hot seat vacated by Raich Carter. However, the directors were not about to be rushed into such a crucial decision. They resisted the temptation to make a panic appointment. Instead they offered the post of caretaker manager to Harold Shepherdson.

There was no risk involved here. Shepherdson had all the necessary qualities to ensure the smooth running of both the club and the team. He was a loyal servant who had seen almost unbroken service with his home-town club since signing professional forms in 1936. Shepherdson was also one of the most respected men in football, having been England trainer during the World Cup win in 1966.

It was no surprise, then, that Shepherdson did a great job in the Boro hot seat as the short-term successor to Anderson. In fact, in a magnificent run from late January until the end of April, Boro lost only three league games during Shep's reign. Without signing any new players, Harold concentrated on teamwork and morale and Boro finished the season like a train, winning their final four games.

As a result, Boro gradually climbed the Second Division table during this three month period and eventually finished in fourth position, just outside the two promotion positions. In modern times, it would have been good enough to earn the club a place in the play-offs.

It was, on reflection, a highly successful playing season. But the fans were not convinced. In fact attendances had plummeted throughout the season and to an average of 10,418, which was a drop of more than 7,500 on the previous year. Gate receipts had dropped dramatically to £55,000 from £97,000. Transfers from that season saw Boro spend £37,000 and bring in £65,000, with the annual wage bill being £86,882. However the club was left with an accumulated deficit of £83,237.

All the more reason then, why the board needed to make the correct decision in finding a new manager in the summer of 1973. If attendances and income did not increase, there would be very little cash available for strengthening the side. If this happened, there was a grave danger that the team would fail to match the achievements of the previous season.

Shepherdson had no intentions of carrying on with the job. He stressed the need for the right man to be appointed on a permanent basis. The fans were crying out for an experienced manager and that was what they expected. But the board went along a different path. They caused something of a surprise when they gave former England International centre-back, Jack Charlton his first stab at football management.

The Ashington-born defender had just ended his illustrious playing career with Leeds United. In a career which spanned almost two decades, Charlton had won all the major honours, including a World Cup winner's medal.

Charlton came from fine stock. His family was related to the famous footballing Milburns, while his brother Bobby, who was a scorer of stunning goals with Manchester United, was an even bigger name in the game than Jack.

Jack's uncle, Jim Milburn, was a full-back with Leeds in the 1950s and had recommended Charlton to the Yorkshire club. He made his league debut in 1953 and went on to notch up a record 629 league appearances for the club. Charlton shared in all of Leeds' domestic and European triumphs in the late 1960s and early 1970s. He won 35 full England caps and, along with Bobby, was in the all-conquering England side which lifted the World Cup. In 1967, he succeeded Bobby as footballer of the year.

It was a terrific pedigree, but Jack Charlton was still an unproven personality in the managerial stakes. On paper, there was no guarantee that he would have the same phenomenal success as a manager which he enjoyed as a player.

That is how the fans must have seen it at the time. They had every right to feel cynical about any new appointment. The name of the Boro was synonymous with 20 years of failure since the club lost its First Division status in the early 1950s. Even with 40-goals-a-season striker Brian Clough in their team, Boro had failed to win promotion. The fans' demands were still very high, but their expectations were fading.

One thing which the fans did not know was that Jack Charlton had no intentions of letting them down. Unproven he may have been as a manager, but Charlton was convinced that he could get the best out of players and turn them into a winning combination. When Charlton came for his interview at Middlesbrough, he admitted later that he had been running the rule over the club, rather than the directors interviewing him. He decided whether he was going to join Boro, and not the other way around. Jack had every intention of being very successful in management and wanted to make sure he was joining a club with genuine potential.

Charlton was true to his word. He turned out to be as strong a character as a manager as he had been as a player on the pitch. Boro's gamble of appointing the World Cup winner went on to pay remarkable dividends. Charlton added the elusive missing ingredients into the Boro side, which

Great to be here: The new Boro boss, accompanied by his wife Pat, arrives at Ayresome Park to begin his managerial career.

were planning and pattern. He introduced a system which suited the strengths of the individuals in his squad and developed a team pattern which mesmerised most of their Second Division opponents.

Charlton also achieved his astonishing success without dipping into the club's coffers. His only experienced signing arrived at Ayresome Park on a free transfer. That free signing was none other than the talented Scottish international midfielder Bobby Murdoch, who made a stunning contribution to the club's rapid march into the First Division.

Otherwise Charlton did not need to use money to bring success to Teesside. He simply moulded the existing players into a team. Jack never spent a single penny in taking Boro into the First Division. And, Charlton didn't merely achieve promotion. He also smashed several records on the way.

So, this is the remarkable story of that incredible season, when Boro swept all before them and had secured promotion before the end of March. The team's wonderful unprecedented all-conquering run from September to April contained just one league defeat, albeit a 5-1 thrashing at Nottingham Forest.

Charlton helped turn many members of the squad which he inherited from Anderson into superstars. Players like Graeme Souness, now regarded as one of the best Scottish midfielders of all time, and the youngster David Armstrong, who went on to play for England.

Naturally the fans came flooding back to Ayresome Park in their droves to see Charlton's Champions stamp great authority on the Second Division. It was one of the club's most memorable seasons in its history.

CHAPTER TWO
THE CAST

MANY people played their part in Boro's amazing success in the 1973-74 season, from the board, with it's new and ambitious chairman Charles Amer, down through the coaching staff to the laundry ladies.

This is a detailed look at the main actors in the story from the public's point of view, namely manager Jack Charlton and all the players who enjoyed a taste of first team action during that memorable time, however brief.

JACK CHARLTON (manager):

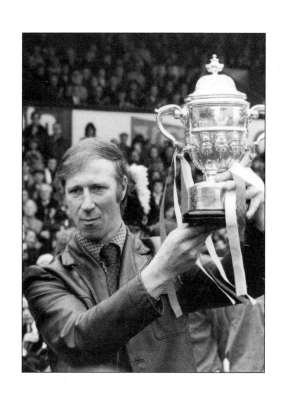

No previous experience. But completely self assured and confident in his abilities to manage. Charlton had just ended a near 20-year love affair with Leeds United when he joined Boro as manager in the summer of 1973.

As a player Jack was tough and uncompromising. He was regarded as a hard competitor and always provided a stiff test for any centre-forward. He made it his business to make sure he got to the ball first.

But anybody who believed that Charlton was just a typical clogging centre-half without any ideas of the intricacies of the game, was in for a shock. The Ashington born boss had an amazing pedigree in the game and soon showed that he had learned from his experiences. Jack proved to be as knowledgeable as any other about how to play the game, and he was a lot more astute than most who crossed his path.

As a player, Charlton had won virtually every British and Continental trophy with which he came into contact. This included a World Cup winner's medal. His successful experiences at Leeds, particularly under the shrewd managership of the wily Don Revie, had helped to nurture the necessary qualities in Jack to ensure that he would take to running a football club like a duck to water.

Above all, Charlton was a winner. Not a born winner. But a self-made winner. This was the whole basis of his character and his personality. He was to stamp it on the Boro first team squad in a big way.

JIM PLATT (goalkeeper):

Brave, courageous and extremely agile, Platt, 21, was the perfect goalkeeper for any team harbouring aspirations of winning promotion.

Like his manager Jack Charlton, Platt came from excellent footballing stock. His father played for Ballymena United and his brother for Cliftonville.

Ironically, Platt was a wing-half at school. When he was with Boro he regularly enjoyed taking a break from his goalkeeper's role to have a run-out around the pitch, particularly in training, where he was said to fancy himself as a goalscorer.

But Jim had made his mind up at the age of 16 that he wanted to develop himself as a goalkeeper, and it did not take him long to break into the Ballymena side.

Ironically, Boro might have lost Platt to Liverpool because it was the Reds who first developed an interest in his burgeoning talents. However Liverpool had just signed Ray Clemence from Scunthorpe United and did not need another young goalkeeper at that time.

It proved to be a decision which was to benefit Boro greatly. Platt won Irish amateur caps and an Irish FA Cup runners-up medal before moving to Teesside in a £7,000 transfer in May, 1970. This fee increased by another £3,000 after Jim had made ten league appearances for the Boro.

However, as far as Boro were concerned, it was money very well spent. Platt went on to prove himself a top quality goalkeeper and quickly displaced Boro's out of form Scottish goalkeeper Willie Whigham in the first team.

In 1971-72, Platt was voted Boro's player of the year. The following season - his first full season in the side - he was an ever present. If Charlton had wanted a better goalkeeper for the job, he would not have found one.

GRAEME SOUNESS (midfield):

A Scot who had everything - brains, brawn, superb ball skills and the ability to score goals. He was also essentially a team player, and developed in leaps and bounds in Charlton's promotion side.

Souness, 20, was arguably Stan Anderson's best ever purchase for the club. But there was a gamble involved at the time because the midfielder had failed to realise all his potential with his original club Tottenham.

Born in Edinburgh, the son of a glazier, Souness was a Scottish schoolboy and youth international who joined Spurs in 1969 and became a full time professional 12 months later. He was a member of the Spurs side which won the FA Youth Cup.

However, like a lot of boys so far from home, Souness suffered from homesickness and returned to Scotland. When he finally went back to Spurs, he found it difficult to make progress because of the hot competition for places.

So, it was with astute timing that Anderson moved in shortly before Christmas in 1972 and paid £32,000 to bring Souness to Teesside. The North-east was closer to the player's Edinburgh home and also provided him with an easier route to first team football.

However, there was no evidence during the summer of 1973 that Souness would become a regular member of Charlton's side, and in fact he was not involved at all in the first three games. Charlton operated with Brian Taylor at centre-back alongside Stuart Boam, with Willie Maddren in midfield.

An injury to Taylor in the fourth game of the season gave Souness the opportunity to come on as substitute in a 1-0 home win against Carlisle United, and he never looked back.

As his confidence grew, the blossoming Souness became a player of great stature, and a key member of the side.

JOHN HICKTON (striker):

Powerful, decisive and with a shot which could rip holes in the back of nets, Hickton, 28, was the archetypal centre-forward. He was a prolific scorer throughout a long and distinguished career with the Boro and his record stands up well against any of the club's other strikers.

Big John was another Stan Anderson signing, being originally signed as a defender to plug the gaps in the early days of the team's season in the Third Division. But he was switched very quickly to a striking role, and never looked back.

Hickton was born in Brimington near Chesterfield, where he was spotted by Sheffield Wednesday. He signed for the Owls in 1962 and, even at that stage, there were doubts about what was his best position.

John scored eight goals in an FA Youth Cuptie when playing as a striker, but it was as a left-back that he made his league debut against Aston Villa in 1964.

Hickton was scoring regularly in the Central League and finally got his chance as a striker in the Wednesday first team, scoring 21 goals in 52 appearanaces, including a hat trick of headers in a match against Arsenal.

However, he was still operating in defensive roles and might have played at centre-half for Wednesday against Everton in the FA Cup Final in 1966. Hickton had deputised on five occasions for regular centre-back Vic Mobley, who was injured, but it was Sam Ellis who earned the nod for the Wembley final.

Shortly following Hickton's Cup Final disappointment, Anderson moved in and paid £20,000 to bring him to Teesside. It turned out to be a magnificent piece of business. Hickton started off in defence, making his Boro debut at centre-back in a 3-2 home win against Workington. He also scored the first of his legendary penalties in that match.

Anderson then moved Hickton to right-back, but after ten matches he was switched up front and scored in a 4-4 draw at Swansea. It was not until near the end of that promotion season that Hickton was finally moved up front on a permanent basis, going on to score 17 goals.

From then on, there was no stopping Hickton. He was Boro's leading scorer for six consecutive seasons. He was top scorer with 15 goals in the season before Charlton's arrival.

ALAN FOGGON (striker):

Bustling runs, a deceptive turn of speed and superb finishing qualities made Foggon the most feared striker in the Second Division after Charlton's arrival on Teesside. Foggon is still often regarded as one of the makeweights in the great Boro side of that era, but in fact he was the jewel in the crown.

Born in West Pelton, Foggon, 23, was a former England youth international. He had joined Newcastle United in 1967 and, as a teenager, played a major part in their Fairs Cup win in 1969. In fact he scored a spectacular goal in the second leg of the final against Ujpest Dozsa.

Foggon went on to score 13 goals for the Magpies in 54 league appearances, but could not establish himself as a permanent fixture in the side. He was transferred to Second Division Cardiff City in August, 1971, and soon found himself embroiled in a relegation battle.

Alan made only 14 appearances for the Bluebirds and it was not the happiest time in his career. Stan Anderson was well aware of Foggon's talents at Newcastle and moved in to bring him back to the North-east in a £10,000 deal in October, 1972. The deal was finally completed after a lot of wrangling between the two clubs.

Foggon had a three-week suspension to serve when he first arrived on Teesside and he did not establish himself in the side until the end of February. He still scored seven goals in 12 starts, plus three as substitute.

When Charlton arrived in the summer, he was looking for a player with pace who could burst through from behind the front two and create havoc in opposition defences. Charlton needed to look no further than his own squad. Foggon was that man. His role in the side ensured that Charlton was able to utilise the perfect system which he had dreamed up for the team.

ERIC McMORDIE (midfield):

Aggressive, courageous and a good ball player, most fans would have expected McMordie, 27, to become a regular in Charlton's midfield. But it did not work out as anticipated.

Born Alexander McMordie in Belfast, but always known as Eric, the midfielder might have joined Manchester United along with fellow Northern Ireland starlet George Best when both lads were 15.

However, McMordie and Best became homseick at Old Trafford and both returned to Ulster. Matt Busby asked both of them to return, but only Best took up the offer.

McMordie went on to play as an amateur for Dundela before he was spotted by Boro's Irish based scout, Matt Willis, and recommended to Raich Carter.

McMordie eventually joined Boro as a professional when he was 18 and managed to settle on Teesside. He made his debut as an inside-forward during the following season, when Boro were relegated from the Second Division. He made a positive contribution to promotion the following year, and it was back in the Second Division when McMordie began to establish himself in the team.

Often fiery, but always hard working and committed, McMordie became a permanent fixture in the side soon afterwards. The first of his 21 Northern Ireland caps came against Israel in 1968.

The season before Charlton's arrival, McMordie lost his place in the February due to a stomach complaint. He started the next season in Charlton's line up, but the signing of Bobby Murdoch effectively put paid to his hopes of a regular place in the side.

WILLIE MADDREN (centre-back):

Cultured, multi talented and a great club man. They called Maddren the best uncapped defender in Britain and few could argue with that description.

But he was also such a good player that he could adapt to any role which was required. In fact Willie initially felt happier playing as a striker, where he believed that his abilities were fully tested. He always said that playing at the back was easy - truly the sign of a top quality player.

Born in Haverton Hill, Maddren, 22, might have joined Leeds United if he had not broken his ankle two days before he was to have a trial at Elland Road. Leeds did not pursue their initial interest and Boro moved in.

Maddren signed professional forms at Ayresome Park in June, 1968, and predictably made his debut as a forward against Bury in the last home game of the season. He had been on the pitch only ten minutes when he broke his nose, but Willie returned to the fray soon after treatment and scored a debut goal.

He was voted player of the year in 1971, by which time he had already proved his versatility by playing in seven different positions for the club.

However it was as a central defender that Maddren was always going to make the biggest impact in the game. After Bill Gates had broken his jaw in an FA Cuptie at Manchester United, Willie stepped into the side and established himself as a permanent fixture.

His continuing versatility led to Charlton using him as a midfielder when the manager first arrived on Teesside. But Willie was quickly moved back to a defensive role, and went on to form a telepathic understanding with Stuart Boam.

STUART BOAM (centre-back):

Tough, uncompromising and rugged. His style was often criticised as unconventional, but few centre-forwards ever came out best from a squirmish with fans' favourite Stuart Boam.

The 25 year old centre-back was born in Kirkby in Ashfield and joined Mansfield Town in 1966, immediately becoming a permanent fixture in the Stags' side. He had already made more than 170 appearances for Mansfield before he came to the attention of the Boro.

Anderson needed a quality centre-back and was prepared to pay the huge sum of £50,000 for the player in May, 1971.

The hard working defender established himself immediately at Ayresome Park and was a regular member of the side for two seasons before Charlton's arrival.

There were one or two problems between Boam and Charlton in the early days of the manager's reign, and it was clear that Stuart was not happy with Jack's forthright criticism of his playing style.

However, the misunderstanding was solved very quickly, Charlton already having indicated his faith in the player by making him skipper at the start of the new season in preference to Willie Maddren. Boam went on to prove that he had all the qualities necessary to become one of the best defenders in the country.

DAVID ARMSTRONG (midfield):

A natural footballer, with vision and an uncanny left foot, Armstrong provided the perfect finishing touch to Charlton's side. At the age of 18, he was also the only teenager in the star studded side.

Armstrong was born in Durham City on Boxing Day in 1954, and was linked to Boro from the age of nine. He became a schoolboy international and joined Boro as an apprentice in June, 1970, eventually becoming a professional 18 months later.

A gifted left sided midfielder, Armstrong was drafted in for his league debut as a 17 year old substitute in a 1-0 defeat at Queens Park Rangers in March, 1972. It was his one and only appearance that season.

The following season Armstrong gradually forced his way into the side, making 19 league appearances, plus another as sub, and scoring his first goal in a 1-1 draw at Aston Villa.

When Charlton took over the reins at Ayresome Park, the teenager was the obvious choice to fulfil the running role up and down the left flank

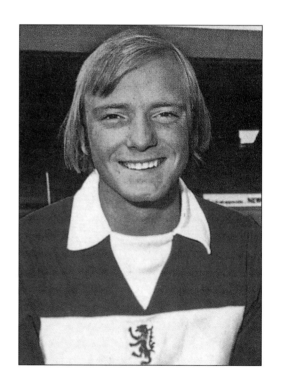

JOHN CRAGGS (right-back):

Strong, determined, a great overlapping full-back with a good crossing ability, Craggsy was a warrior. He was the kind of player you needed whenever there was a battle on.

It was no surprise that Charlton went on to describe him as the best attacking full-back in the business. Craggs, 24, possessed a great shot, and was a precision passer of the ball. But the full-back was just as well known for his aggression and competitive spirit.

John was a Stan Anderson signing in August, 1971. The then Boro boss paid Newcastle United £60,000 for his services. It was regarded as a high fee at the time, specially considering that Craggs had made only 50 appearances for the Magpies.

Craggs' problem at St James's Park was that he was permanently in the shadow of David Craig, and never really had the opportunity to establish himself as a serious first team contender on Tyneside.

When Charlton arrived at Ayresome Park, Craggs was already an regular member of the side. In two seasons, he had missed just two games. John had all the experience that Charlton needed to make the right-back spot his own in the Dream Team.

FRANK SPRAGGON (left-back):

Dependable, committed and experienced, Spraggon, 28, had already been at Ayresome Park for more than ten years when Big Jack arrived.

The son in law of Harold Shepherdson, Frank was born at Marley Hill and was signed for Boro by Bob Dennison in 1962.

He quickly pushed his way through the junior sides and made his debut the following year, going on to establish himself as Boro's regular left-half for several seasons.

The season 1971-72 was not a good one for Spraggon when a cartilage operation and then trouble with blurred vision kept him on the sidelines for seven months.

The emergence of Willie Maddren was a major threat to Frank's place in the side, but he made a successful transition to left-back when Gordon Jones retired.

Spraggon had been operating in the No.3 shirt for a full season when Charlton joined Boro, and comfortably held on to the position as Big Jack assembled his line-up for the promotion assault.

BOBBY MURDOCH (midfield):

Ball player extraordinary, a great reader of the game and a superb link-up man. Murdoch had been displaying these uncanny talents with Glasgow Celtic for several years before agreeing to become Jack Charlton's first signing on a free transfer in September, 1973.

Born in Bothwell in Lanarkshire, Murdoch, 29, had forged a reputation for himself as a brilliant attacking inside-forward.

Overall he spent 14 years at Parkhead and was regarded as one of Scotland's most influential players in the 1960s. He had helped Celtic to win seven league championships as well as successes in the Scottish FA and League Cups.

The midfielder had been capped 12 times by his country and was voted Scotland's player of the year in 1969. However his crowning glory came as a member of the Celtic side which became the first British club to win the European Cup in 1967.

It was something of a scoop when Charlton snapped up Murdoch on a free, even though the player had lost a lot of his mobility. His ball playing skills, however, were as good as ever.

Murdoch made his Boro debut in a goalless draw at Blackpool towards the end of September, before scoring on his home debut in a 2-0 win against Bristol City. He made a remarkable impression on Charlton's young side.

DAVID MILLS (striker):

Pacey, skilful and self motivated, Mills was one of those talented players who seemed to get better every season. His contribution to the fortunes of his home town club over several years was massive.

Mills, 21, was born in Whitby but was brought up in Thornaby, where his achievements earned him English schoolboy international caps.

The big clubs were queuing up for his signature as a young player, and Manchester United were one of the clubs very interested. However Mills suffered a back injury which kept him out of football for a full year, and the interest waned.

Once the teenager was back in action, Boro moved in quickly and Mills signed up at Ayresome Park at the same time as Willie Maddren, in July 1968. He was only 17 when he made his first team debut as a substitute at Birmingham City in 1969.

The following season Mills scored on his full debut in a 3-0 win at Swindon Town, having earlier made several more appearances as sub.

David gradually began to establish himself, though he was far from prolific in his early days and scored just five goals in 37 league appearances in the season before Charlton took over the reins at Ayresome Park.

However, Charlton's influence was the making of Mills as a fully fledged striker and the player gradually gained in stature, playing a vital role in the promotion line-up.

BILL GATES (centre-back):

Hard, tough, uncompromising and a great team man, Gates was in the swansong of an illustrious career when Charlton arrived.

Ferryhill-born Gates, 29, captained the England youth team before joining Boro as an amateur in 1959. He was such an outstanding prospect that he made his Boro debut when he was still only 16 and a pupil at Spennymoor Grammar School.

In the 1961-62 season, Gates played 14 games in two separate runs in the team. He had been torn between becoming a professional footballer or following a career as an accountant, but eventually decided to chance his luck with the Boro and turned pro that season.

During his 13-year stay with the club, Gates experienced fluctuating fortunes, but he went on to make more than 300 appearances, mostly at centre-half.

He suffered a double fracture of his jaw during an FA Cuptie at Manchester United but made a full recovery and continued to display the same resolution and commitment every time that he took to the pitch.

In 1972-73 Bill did not push his way into the team until late September, but went on to play a big part, scoring three goals in 33 league appearances. His final goal for the club came in a 3-0 home win against Sheffield Wednesday in the April.

MALCOLM SMITH (striker):

Fearless and fervent, Smith worked very hard to try to oust the experienced strikers who were in front of him in Charlton's side.

The 19 year old from Stockton had signed professional forms in 1970 and made his debut in a 3-0 home win against Hull City in the final game of the 1971-72 season.

The following season he was drafted straight into the side and celebrated with a dream start, grabbing both goals in a 2-1 derby win against Sunderland at Ayresome Park.

Smith went on to score six goals that season in 19 appearances, plus another five as substitute, which gave him the experience and confidence to fulfil an excellent job for Charlton whenever required.

BRIAN TAYLOR (centre-back):

Raw, but determined, Taylor might well have gone on to become a lynchpin in Charlton's side if things had worked out differently.

The 19 year old centre-back, who was born in Hodthorpe, was one of the players who impressed Charlton with his hard work and commitment in training in the summer of 1973.

The teenager had made four appearances in the previous season, and started out as Charlton's first choice centre-back alongside new skipper Stuart Boam, with Willie Maddren operating in midfield.

However, Taylor was injured in his fourth game under Charlton, Maddren was moved further back, and the lad never got the chance to re-establish himself.

PETER BRINE (midfield):

Lively and enterprising, Brine was battling to try to break into the Boro first team when Charlton arrived at Ayresome Park.

The Londonder, 20, had joined Boro in July, 1968, and was working hard to push himself up through the ranks.

Brine, who could play up front or in midfield, made his debut for Boro as a substitute in a 1-0 home win against Millwall in October, 1972. He scored his first goal for the club in a 2-0 win against Cardiff the following March and made ten appearances that season, half of them when coming off the bench.

HARRY CHARLTON (midfield):

Busy and resolute, Harry was on the fringe of the first team when Jack Charlton took over the helm.

The 22 year old from Gateshead had made his debut in the 1970-71 season when he played four consecutive games. However he failed to feature at all in the side the following season.

Charlton, no relation to the Boro manager, opened the 1972-73 season in the team and played in the first three games. But once again he was unable to hang on to his spot, and no doubt was hoping that a change of manager might improve his fortunes.

PETER CREAMER (right-back):

Cool, calm and collected, Creamer was a talented young defender but his route to the first team was blocked by John Craggs.

Creamer, 19, was born in Hartlepool and turned professional in October, 1970. He made his debut at left-back in a 2-1 home defeat by Fulham in August, 1972, and went on to make seven appearances that season, including one as substitute in the League Cup second replay at Tottenham.

JIMMY COCHRANE
(left-back):

Workmanlike and assiduous, Cochrane, 19, was still awaiting his league debut when Charlton took over.

Born in Glasgow, Cochrane was signed from Drumchapel Amateurs in May, 1971, and was a promising left-back.

PAT CUFF
(goalkeeper):

A great shot stopper and brave keeper, Cuff, 21, had been a professional for four years in the summer of 1973.

The Middlesbrough born player was still awaiting his first team debut, having found it difficult to oust established keeper Jim Platt.

MALCOLM POSKETT
(striker):

A clinical finisher, Poskett, 20, had just been snapped up from local club South Bank when Charlton. arrived.

TONY McANDREW
(centre-back):

A strapping and brave defender, McAndrew was one of Boro's very promising youngsters in the summer of 1973.

The 17 year old from Lanark had earned Scottish youth international honours shortly after joining Boro in July, 1971.

CHAPTER THREE
JULY & AUGUST

The big build up

BORO were among the favourites to win the Second Division Championship at the start of the 1973-74 season, though FA Cup Winners Sunderland and Aston Villa headed the betting.

Local bookmaker Dennis Maxwell quoted Boro at 12-1 to win the league and 3-1 to finish anywhere in the top three.

It was to be the first season where the three-up three-down rule was to apply between First and Second Division clubs.

Boro were hoping for a good start to improve attendances at Ayresome Park, and the cost of entry had been fixed at: South Terrace standing 45p, elsewhere 40p, Boys End 20p. Seats, 60p, 70p + 80p. Season ticket prices were £14 for an adult, £7.50 for children.

Pre-season training started officially on Wednesday, July 18, although all players had been "invited" to report in twice a week in the closed season, five times a week if they chose, with Charlton saying: "There is no reason for any player to sit around getting fat."

PRE-SEASON FRIENDLY RESULTS

SATURDAY JULY 28
Morton 0, Middlesbrough 2

Platt, Craggs, Spraggon, Boam, Taylor, Maddren, McMordie, Mills, Hickton, Foggon, Armstrong.

Scorer: Mills 2.

MONDAY JULY 30
Hamilton Academicals 1, Middlesbrough 3

Cuff, Craggs, Spraggon, Boam, Taylor, Stiles, Maddren, H.Charlton, Hickton, Foggon, Armstrong.

Scorers: Craggs, Armstrong, Hickton.

WEDNESDAY AUGUST 1
Partick Thistle 0, Middlesbrough 2

Platt, Craggs, Spraggon, Boam, Taylor, Maddren, McMordie, Foggon, Hickton, Smith, Armstrong.

Scorers: McMordie, Brine.

SATURDAY AUGUST 11
Middlesbrough 1, Newcastle United 3

Platt, Craggs, Spraggon, Boam, Taylor, Maddren, McMordie, Mills, Hickton, Foggon, Armstrong.

Scorer: Mills.

SATURDAY AUGUST 18
York City 2 Middlesbrough 1

Platt, Craggs, Souness, Boam, Gates, Maddren, McMordie, Stiles, Hickton, Mills, Armstrong.

Scorer: Mills.

MONDAY AUGUST 20
Grimsby Town 1 Middlesbrough 2

Platt, Craggs, Spraggon, Boam, Taylor, Maddren, McGivern, Mills, Hickton, Foggon, Armstrong.

Scorers: Foggon, Hickton.

Nobby Stiles, left, soon to be transferred to Preston, and David Armstrong organise the defence in the pre-season friendly against Hamilton Accies.

It's August 1973 and Jack Charlton unveils his squad for the forthcoming promotion campaign.

Selection Headaches

THE build up to the Boro's opening game of the season was far from smooth. Nobby Stiles was still club captain, despite his insistence that he needed to leave the club for personal reasons. He would have played at Fratton Park had he not sustained a cut foot during a reserve game against Grimsby the previous Monday. The wound needed two stitches and Stiles didn't travel south with the squad.

Graeme Souness had missed training the previous Wednesday suffering with a back strain, Eric McMordie was having constant treatment on a niggling groin strain, Willie Maddren had a sore knee, while Frank Spraggon had a leg complaint. It left Charlton with a selection headache as he prepared for his managerial bow.

By contrast, Portsmouth intended parading three new signings. Peter Marinello, a tricky ball player, was a £100,000 capture from Arsenal, while fellow striker Ron Davies was a £60,000 arrival from neighbours Southampton and defender Phil Roberts had come from Bristol Rovers for £55,000. All three were expected to pull on a Pompey shirt for the first time and there were high hopes on the South Coast that the trio might help spark a fine season.

Charlton was forced to leave it late to name his team and even later to name a new skipper.

In the absence of Stiles. Many expected Maddren to be given the honour of leading the side. The all-rounder was an experienced and respected member of the team and had qualities necessary to skipper the side.

Stuart Boam had spent the summer wondering if he would be in the side, especially as he was playing in a position which Charlton had made his own for 12 years at Leeds.

One of the first things Charlton had done when taking over was to get all the lads together to see what they were made of. There were occasional press reports that he didn't like what he saw in Boam and he had told him so in no uncertain terms, on more than one occasion.

Imagine the surprise when it was the much maligned - if only by Charlton - Boam who was named as the man who would lead the team. It turned out to be an excellent choice, and the player who gave him most support during the season was fellow defender Maddren.

* * * * *

SATURDAY AUGUST 25
Portsmouth 0   Middlesbrough 1

PORTSMOUTH	MIDDLESBROUGH
Tilsed	Platt
Roberts	Craggs
Wilson	Spraggon
Piper	McMordie
Stephenson	Boam
Munks	Taylor
Marinello	Maddren
Kellard	Hickton (Smith 59)
Davies	Mills
Foggo (Lewis 64)	Foggon
Price	Armstrong

Scorer: Foggon 21.

Attendance: 19,799.

Match Report

THIS was a game of firsts. The opening match of the 1973-74 season not only saw new players, on the Portsmouth side anyway, but new chairmen and new managers.

John Deacon and Charles Amer were introduced to John Mortimore and Jack Charlton, the new players and the crowd, before the kick-off.

Eighty degree heat bathed Fratton Park as Middlesbrough, including McMordie, Spraggon and Maddren, but not Souness, were forced on to the back foot under immediate Portsmouth pressure. The anticipation was high, and the crowd gave the home side superb backing as Pompey surged forward in the opening stages.

Jim Platt was called into action early in the game as Ron Davies threatened with a header, while the speed of Peter Marinello caused problems.

However, the crowd were silenced when Boro took the lead against the run of play. Maddren, looking calm and composed in midfield, fed McMordie. His first time cross was measured to reach Alan Foggon, who beat Ron Tilsed with a glancing header which went in off the post with just 21 minutes gone.

The goal seemed to boost Boro and they went on to take command. Tilsed came too far off his line and David Mills, showing great awareness, shot for goal. However, the ball took a deflection and went behind for a corner.

Boro continued to press and McMordie dispossessed left-back Billy Wilson only to shoot wide.

McMordie then sent Mills clear, but he let the ball run too far and Tilsed came out smartly to gather.

Portsmouth seemed to gather their thoughts - and a rocket from Mortimore - at half-time and flew at Boro in the early exchanges of the second 45 minutes.

Davies headed against the bar, then set up inside-forward Bobby Kellard with a chance which he sent just wide.

Boro broke free from the pressure. Mills raced clear and sent over a deep cross which Tilsed missed. McMordie and John Hickton both raced in to get a touch which would have brought a goal, both missing by inches.

Brian Taylor, who had been selected as first choice centre-half, sent over a cross which set up McMordie, but a mis-kick from the Irishman wasted a good opportunity.

A limping Hickton left the pitch after straining a calf muscle on the hour and was replaced by Malcolm Smith who had started only one of Boro's six pre-season friendlies.

Pompey stretched Boro for the final half hour and should have equalised when Stuart Boam lost the ball in the sun, and Davies found Norman Piper, only to watch in anguish as the wing-half, unmarked, shot wide.

- MAN OF THE MATCH -

LEGEND Jimmy Dickinson, who played 764 league games for Portsmouth, gave his vote to STUART BOAM, saying: "I wouldn't say he has all the finesse in the world, but he is big and commanding."

The distinctive banded shirt, which was to become synonymous with the Charlton era, receives the official seal of approval from Portsmouth Man of the Match, Stuart Boam, centre, John Hickton and Jack Charlton.

Pointing the way to the First Division is Middlesbrough FC chairman Charles Amer, centre, with fellow directors, left to right, Mr G.B. Wood, Mr J.D. Hatfield, Dr U.N. Phillips, Mr E. Varley, Mr G.T. Kitching, Mr M. McCullough and Mr J.E. Thomas.

REFLECTIONS

David Mills

IT wasn't just a special season for David Mills, it was a pretty special year. Promotion, international honours and marriage, but maybe not in that order of importance!

"It was an incredible time in so many ways," he says, reflecting fondly. "Obviously the marriage had been known about at the turn of the year, but there was no indication about what was going to happen on the footballing front."

It was David's fourth full season with the club and he, despite the critics, had become a very useful player.

"As a footballer you will always have critics, no matter who you are. I had them, but they didn't bother me that much. As long as I was playing every week I knew I must be doing something right. I missed very few games that season, but those I did miss were through injury. I was never dropped and I think that told its own story.

"That was the biggest accolade I received from Jack Charlton, that he kept me in the side."

Mills in fact missed only four league games, becoming an integral part in a team of regulars.

He said: "When you look back it was amazing that we didn't have too many injuries and that had to be a factor in our success.

"That and the ability to score goals from anywhere on the field. How many sides then, or since then, have had forwards who were good for 30 goals a season between them, midfield players who would chip in with 35 and defenders who could score ten or so?

"If we were kept quiet up front, then there were players right across the pitch who were just as likely to pop up and score."

The reason behind the success?

"Jack Charlton and some very good players.

"Jack's influence was of course significant, very significant, but he couldn't have done what he did with players who couldn't play. He knew when he joined the club that he was taking over a useful outfit.

"He was very shrewd. He had us watched a couple of times and must have known he had a fine chance of making it work when he moved into management. He got the blend and the balance right and had quality players to work with."

It was the almost self-centred approach of Charlton which brought him success. At least that is the view of Mills.

"Retrospectively you look and realise what he was doing and the way he did it. His approach was that he would do things his own way. That way if he got the sack he couldn't blame anybody else!

"It was difficult at first to get used to what he wanted. We didn't always agree. Not many of us liked training on a Saturday morning before the match for instance, but it was difficult to argue. What he was doing was bringing us success."

It was a year which brought personal success for Mills, as well the team recognition.

He scored the goal which won Boro the championship at Luton - "Obviously my most special memory of that season" - as well as gaining international recognition.

"I was chosen to play for the England Under-23 side and did well. I was then chosen to go on tour with them at the end of the season. As soon as I came back from that, after doing well again, I was told I was joining up with the full squad. I couldn't believe it. It was great at the time and gives me good memories now."

Mills was regarded by many as the fittest player at the club, but there was more to his game than just running.

"We all had a job to do, mine was to give the midfield lads an option. Bobby Murdoch was probably the finest passer of the ball in the game at that time, but he didn't hit every single pass to my feet. He knew that if he played the ball into space I would be there challenging. It sometimes made his bad passes look good!

"It wasn't all that much to look at maybe, but it was part of our team's success. We all worked for each other, all the time, and we knew if we did that then we stood every chance of success.

"The quality of the side was such that we never struggled, or came close to struggling, even when we were playing in a higher division the next year."

CHAPTER FOUR
SEPTEMBER

– NEWS UPDATE –

Stiles out....Souness back

THERE was little time for reflection on the Monday morning after the game as Charlton was busy in the transfer market, selling Nobby Stiles to Preston North End, who were managed by brother Bobby.

Stiles had cost Boro £25,000 when signing from Manchester United two years earlier, replacing Gordon Jones as captain.

But his wife had found it difficult to settle on Teesside and wanted to move to Sale in Cheshire.

She had all but sold the family house in Yarm and Nobby had been requesting a move for quite some time.

Charlton said: "I'm sorry to let Nobby go. I wanted to keep the Nobby Stiles I remembered and I always said that I wouldn't let him go until an adequate replacement had been found.

"Well now I've found one. Willie Maddren is performing very well in midfield and we have to give youngsters like him a chance at this club.

"We have a few more who are in mind, players like Tony McAndrew, Jimmy Cochrane and Harry Charlton."

Stiles, who had given Boro two years' good service despite losing some of his mobility, was sold for £20,000.

* * * * *

No kick and run

GRAEME Souness had returned to training on the Monday and played for the reserves the following night.

Boro beat Grimsby Town in the first leg of the North Midland League Cup Final with goals from Souness and Malcolm Poskett, yet still came in for criticism from supporters who branded the football played as "boring", a tag which was to follow Boro's senior squad around the country. However it was one which was hardly justified.

Doubtless a few of the Boro season-ticket holders at the reserve match were not in the best of moods anyway after being told they would have to pay to get in because, in the words of the club: "This was a game which was held over from last season, therefore this seasons tickets are not valid!"

The response to the fans' criticism was sharp from Charlton as he said: "We are not going to play pit-yard kick and run football. The players at this club are playing to instructions. My instructions. If the fans have a problem with that then they should see me!"

The record shows that not many, if any, took up the offer.

* * * * *

League Cup draw

THE draw for the second round of the League Cup was made on the Wednesday prior to Boro's opening home game of the season against Fulham.

The club were drawn away in every cup match they played that season. Their first port of call was Old Trafford and a game against a struggling Manchester United side. It was the sixth time the clubs had been drawn against each other in three and a half years.

"I don't care," was the response from Charlton, on hearing the news. "I think anyone has a chance of beating them the way they are playing at the moment. Anyway I'm more concerned about this Saturday's match."

Of chief concern to Charlton were injuries to Boam and Hickton. The latter had limped off at Portsmouth with a calf strain and had not trained for most of the week, while Boam had severe bruising to a big toe damaged in training on the Tuesday.

To the relief of all concerned, both were passed fit and the intentions of Charlton to keep a settled side were made clear when he said: "I feel it is very important to have a settled side so early in the season. It helps achieve a balance and a rhythm."

Charlton appealed to fans who had stayed away in the previous seasons to come back to the club, saying simply: "If you're not doing anything on Saturday, we'd love to see you."

Fulham manager Alec Stock, speaking from Craven Cottage on the banks of the Thames, knew what sort of match it was going to be. He had prepared his team well, saying: "It will be a hard game. It's never anything else up at Middlesbrough, but we beat Millwall 2-0 last week and I'm not going up there to kiss them!"

Prior to the game Boro announced the signing of a 19 year old winger from Manchester United called Frank McGivern.

McGivern was educated in Middlesbrough, having attended St Anthony's School, moving to United afterwards. He failed to make the breakthrough at Old Trafford and also with Boro, never making a first team appearance.

* * * * *

SATURDAY SEPTEMBER 1

Middlesbrough 0	Fulham 2

MIDDLESBROUGH	**FULHAM**
Platt	Mellor
Craggs	Cutbush
Spraggon	Slough
Taylor	Mullery
Boam	Went
Maddren	Dunne
McMordie (Smith 72)	Conway
Armstrong	Earle
Mills	Busby
Hickton	Lloyd
Foggon	Barrett
	Sub: Moreline

Scorers: Barrett 70, Earle 75.
Attendance: 14,976.

Match Report

BOTH Boro and Fulham were unchanged from their opening outings for the season's first home game which was played under a blazing sun.

Eric McMordie was prominent in the early exchanges, setting up Alan Foggon with a chance which was wasted by poor control.

Attacking full-back John Craggs was quick to send striker David Mills clear. Mills' pace took him well beyond his nearest marker, but also away from any Boro player who may have latched on to his cross.

Boro 'keeper Jim Platt was called into play, superbly saving a close range drive from Jim Conway, but it was Fulham goalkeeper Peter Mellor who was the busiest man on the pitch as Boro poured forward, Mellor almost being beaten by a low drive from left-back Frank Spraggon.

The clash had developed into an all action game. Midfielder David Armstrong beat four Fulham players before firing in a fierce drive which was held by Mellor, who was also on hand to produce a fine save from a John Hickton first time effort.

Boro forced four corners in quick succession, failing to make any of them count, and had to scarper back quickly as Fulham broke, centre-half Brian Taylor bringing down Les Cutbush to become the first Boro player booked in the season.

Mills hit the post after 68 minutes but Fulham hit the back of the net two minutes later.

Craggs was dispossessed by winger Les Barrett, who cut inside the penalty area and hammered a shot past Platt.

Striker Malcolm Smith replaced McMordie two minutes later, but it was Fulham who wrapped up the points with their second goal on 75 minutes.

Barrett was involved again. He raced clear down Boro's right, sending over a good cross, and Steve Earle left Platt helpless with a close range header.

Boro had a chance to reduce the arrears ten minutes from time, but Hickton headed wide of an empty net.

– MAN OF THE MATCH –

THE Fulham manager Alec Stock gave the award to DAVID ARMSTRONG, reasoning: "I could only give it on Boro's first-half performance. Armstrong deserved to win it. I liked his attitude, he was full of running and caused us quite a bit of trouble with long diagonal passes."

The calm experience of former England international, Alan Mullery (above), certainly contributed to Fulham's surprising victory at Ayresome Park.

– NEWS UPDATE –

Sorry

FOLLOWING the poor result against Fulham, Jack Charlton said he felt sorry for Boro's fans. He blasted his team when saying: "They were good enough to come and support us and they had to watch that.

"It was a lively game for quite a spell, but we lost our way towards the end. I have some convincing to do. I have to convince the fans that we deserve their support and I have to convince the players that my ideas are better than their ideas.

"That is why they will be in for training morning and afternoon this coming week. There were times on Saturday when we were unbelievably bad."

Alec Stock admitted after the game: "Boro were better in the first half. We had a right old swearing match at half-time and we were better in the second!"

The worrying factor for Charlton was the way Boro faded noticeably in the closing stages.

* * * * *

First trophy

BORO'S first trophy of the season came on Tuesday, September 4, although technically it was a throwback to the previous season.

Taking a 2-0 lead from the first-leg, Boro's reserves completed a 4-1 aggregate win over Grimsby to win the North Midland League Cup thanks to goals from Malcolm Poskett and Graeme Souness, the same scorers as in the first game at Ayresome Park.

Souness, needing to step up his fitness level, came on as a substitute, but played again the next night when part of a team captained by John Hickton which won a five-a-side tournament at Thornaby Pavilion.

Boro fielded two teams for the event which also included a team from Sunderland involving players who had been part of the Roker side's FA Cup winning side four months earlier.

Jimmy Montgomery, Vic Halom, Denis Tueart, Billy Hughes and Cup winning captain Bobby Kerr formed a team which didn't even make the final of this competition.

Darlington were captained by former Boro skipper Gordon Jones, but it was the two Middlesbrough teams which contested the final.

Harry Charlton scored twice and goalkeeper Jim Platt, playing outfield, grabbed the other as Hickton's side won 3-1.

Jimmy Cochrane scored for the other Boro side, captained by Stuart Boam.

The sides were:

Winners: Cuff, Harry Charlton, Souness, Mills, Hickton, Platt.

Runners-up: Gormley, Craggs, Boam, Gates, Maddren, Foggon, Cochrane.

Harry Charlton was voted player of the tournament and brought the following praise from Jack Charlton: "Harry Charlton, what a footballer. He's going to do a lot for Middlesbrough."

Charlton also bore reference to Souness, saying: "His application is so much improved."

* * * * *

To the Palace

WILLIE Maddren had an injection to dispel some congealed blood on the outside of his right knee, while Malcolm Smith had a slight ankle knock, so Peter Brine was named as a substitute ahead of Graeme Souness for Boro's next game, away to Crystal Palace.

The South London club, under the managership of the flamboyant Malcolm Allison, had spent a lot of money putting their side together and were getting no return.

Goalkeeper Paul Hammond was dropped after conceding five goals in two games, John Jackson returned, while there was no place for the club skipper Paddy Mulligan. Charlie Cooke was left out of a side which had lost its opening two games.

Boro were unchanged for the third game in a row and were given salt tablets before playing a game in tremendous heat.

* * * * *

We are the Champions: A sign of things to come as Boro's A squad, left to right, Cuff, Charlton, Mills, Hickton, Souness and Platt "proudly" display the club's first trophy of the year. Also pictured is the fans' favourite adopted uncle, the Evening Gazette's sports editor Cliff Mitchell.

SATURDAY SEPTEMBER 8
Crystal Palace 2   Middlesbrough 3

CRYSTAL PALACE	MIDDLESBROUGH
Jackson	Platt
Roffey	Craggs
Taylor	Spraggon
Cannon	Boam
Bell	Taylor
Blyth	Maddren
Possee	McMordie
Walley	Mills
Whittle	Hickton
Chatterton	Foggon
Rogers	Armstrong
Sub: Phillip	Sub: Brine

Scorers: Hickton 8, Craggs o.g. 64, Mills 66, Taylor 69,
        Cannon 76.

Attendance: 17,554.

*Just over a decade after this defeat, the outspoken Palace
manager, Malcolm Allison (above), would be in the
Ayresome Park hot seat. He would, however, be unable to
halt the Boro's catastrophic slide towards liquidation.*

Match Report

EARLY Boro pressure paid off after just eight minutes. David
Armstrong pushed the ball out wide, John Hickton held off a
challenge from Bobby Bell and neatly slid his low drive under
John Jackson.

Boro almost made it two when Hickton set up David Mills, a
fierce drive cracking back off the crossbar. Palace hit back and a
snap shot from Mel Blyth caused Jim Platt problems. The ball
bounced off the chest of the Boro 'keeper, but was gathered at
the second attempt.

Palace applied the pressure at the start of the second half and
John Craggs had to clear as Platt could only parry a piledriver
from Alan Whittle. The Palace team argued that the ball had gone
over the line, but the referee was having none of it.

The home side did draw level after 64 minutes. Blyth sent over a
high cross and Craggs, attempting to head clear, diverted the ball
into his own net.

It took Boro just two minutes to regain the lead. Eric McMordie
split the Palace defence apart, and Hickton raced away and sent
over a fine cross which Mills hammered in from close range.

Boro wrapped things up with the game's third goal in five
minutes. A shot from Mills was beaten out by Jackson, a follow
up from Foggon was bundled clear, but only to Brian Taylor, who
scored his first goal for the club.

Taylor and Palace winger Derek Possee were lying prostrate in
the penalty area, possibly blocking Platt's view, when Jim Cannon
netted with a speculative long range effort after 76 minutes as
the scoring continued. But the Scot's effort proved to be the last
of the game.

Palace manager Malcolm Allison described Boro as "the best team
we have played this season", while Jack Charlton said: "Every
player worked himself into the ground. We won and I can smile,
but it is the easiest thing in the world to smile when you win.

"Nobody would have recognised us as the side which lost to
Fulham, but we seem to play better away from home."

– MAN OF THE MATCH –

*CRYSTAL Palace manager Malcolm Allison nominated
two players, DAVID ARMSTRONG and DAVID MILLS.
"Armstrong, he made telling runs, used the ball well and
is a fine prospect. Mills has a more difficult role. He does
a tremendous amount of running and showed good skill.
I couldn't split the pair."*

– NEWS UPDATE –

Table Toppers

BORO knew they would go joint top of the table if they won their next game, at home to Carlisle United.

There was only one doubt for the match, but Charlton was able to name another unchanged side after Hickton, kicked in the face at Palace, declared himself fit.

Graeme Souness had reported back overweight from the summer break and had only started one friendly game when he was taken off after 43 minutes when playing at left-back at York.

However he was named as substitute ahead of Brine, while Carlisle made two changes to the side which had beaten Notts County the previous Saturday.

Striker Bob Owen failed a fitness test, teenager Mick Barry, a £40,000 signing from Huddersfield, took his place, while Stan Ternent was preferred to Roger Delgado.

Former Boro player Joe Laidlaw was in the United side, while Boro's coach Ian MacFarlane had been sacked as Carlisle manager less than two years previously.

*   *   *   *   *

TUESDAY SEPTEMBER 11

Middlesbrough 1   Carlisle United 0

MIDDLESBROUGH	CARLISLE UNITED
Platt	Ross
Craggs	Carr
Spraggon	Gorman
Boam	Ternent
Taylor (Souness 10)	Green
Maddren	Tiler
McMordie	O'Neill
Mills	Barry
Hickton	Clarke
Foggon	Laidlaw
Armstrong	Martin
	Sub: Owen

Scorer: Craggs 71.

Attendance: 16,837.

– MAN OF THE MATCH –

THE Carlisle manager Alan Ashman nominated ALAN FOGGON and JOHN CRAGGS.
Ashman said: "Foggon continually ran at our defence and it could have caused more trouble than it did. As for John Craggs, he was very effective defensively and he deserved a nomination for that goal!"

Match Report

BORO'S first home win of the season was hard fought and came in unspectacular fashion.

There was little to comment on throughout the 90 minutes, although Boro, after a half-time roasting from Jack Charlton, were better in the second 45 minutes.

Carlisle defended desperately and played a lot of negative football. Back-passing was allowed that season and Boro used the tactic a lot. However, Carlisle played the tactic to perfection, constantly frustrating Boro and a near 17,000 crowd.

Brian Taylor was injured after only ten minutes. The teenager's left eye was completely closed after contact from the elbow of Joe Laidlaw. That proved to be the last game Taylor would play that season.

Although recovering from the injury after a week or so, Taylor's place in the back four had been taken by Willie Maddren and, after starting the season as the first choice centre-half, Taylor wasn't seen again until the opening game of the following season.

Maddren dropped into the back four with Graeme Souness coming on as a substitute to play in a first team game for the first time in over five months.

Boro's winner came after 71 minutes, direct from a free-kick. Carlisle put five men in a defensive wall, Stuart Boam standing on the end. John Craggs aimed the free-kick at Boam from just outside the penalty area. The skipper moved out of the way just in time and the ball whistled into the bottom corner.

Boro should have made it two after David Mills was brought down inside the penalty area, but John Hickton missed from the spot with 12 minutes remaining.

An injury to the unlucky Brian Taylor, caused by the elbow of ex-Boro forward Joe Laidlaw, left, resulted in the enforced positional changes which were to ironically strengthen Middlesbrough's promotion campaign.

– NEWS UPDATE –

Carlisle Reaction

THE result was good enough to put Boro joint top of the table.

Charlton's reaction? "I was pleased with the result, but not overwhelmed with the performance."

As for Hickton and what was a rare penalty miss, he said: "Lack of practice, but that's the time to miss, when it doesn't affect the result!"

Charlton had more than one complaint on the night, as well as his team's performance. He complained about the "inadequacy" of the PA system.

He added: "I sympathise with our crowd. You can't hear a thing. It's OK when there is nobody in the ground! We need to work on it."

* * * * *

Club Shop

CHARLTON was determined to be involved in all aspects of the club, not just the playing side, and announced that he and his wife were to oversee the opening of a club shop.

Charlton's wife, Pat, said: "Jack and I ran shops for five years at Leeds. Leeds couldn't make a success of them, so Jack and I built them up to quite a size and Leeds took them back!

"We are having a few problems here. We are having trouble getting things made with Boro on them. Everyone wants us to buy in bulk and that is not feasible at the moment."

* * * * *

Top of the table clash

JOINT leaders Aston Villa were the next visitors to Ayresome. Villa, many people's choice as promotion candidates, had started well. They had remained unchanged for their opening four games, taking six points. This, despite playing without the previous season's leading scorer Ray Graydon, as well as Chico Hamilton and Sammy Morgan, a 6' 2" centre-forward signed in the close season from Port Vale for £25,000.

"I'd have preferred to play them later in the season when we had settled down," admitted Charlton beforehand.

"But I think this will be a cracker. The crowd were right behind us on Tuesday and we call on their support again. I know the public in Middlesbrough may take some convincing that we can be a good team, but I would ask them to come and watch us and see for themselves."

Charlton was forced into making his first team change of the season as Brian Taylor had failed to recover from the blow in the eye taken against Carlisle.

Boro started with the side which played the final 80 minutes of that game, with Willie Maddren dropping into the back four and Graeme Souness in midfield.

* * * * *

SATURDAY SEPTEMBER 15
Middlesbrough 0   Aston Villa 0

MIDDLESBROUGH	ASTON VILLA
Platt	Cumbes
Craggs	Robson
Spraggon	Aitken
Souness	Rioch
Boam	Nicholl
Maddren	Ross
McMordie (Brine 53)	Brown
Mills	Hockey
Hickton	Evans
Foggon	Vowden
Armstrong	Little
	Sub: Graydon

Attendance: 19,656.

Match Report

JOHN Craggs was first to pose any threat, having a 20 yard drive blocked, while Boro had penalty appeals turned down when Alan Foggon was checked inside the area.

Boro began to step up the pressure, Jimmy Cumbes saving a John Hickton header, while David Mills miskicked in front of goal and then shot inches wide.

Foggon set off on a quick break, spreading the ball wide to Hickton. His first time cross was sent over the bar by Eric McMordie. A snap shot from David Armstrong was saved by Cumbes, while the Villa 'keeper kept up his outstanding display by denying another Boro chance after a mis-cue from Ian Ross.

Villa broke and created a clear chance, but Brian Little failed to make good contact and Boro hit back. Armstrong grazed the bar and Mills hit the post before Bruce Rioch sent John Robson away on the break, his shot being tipped over the bar by Jim Platt, with Craggs clearing off the line minutes later.

The longer the game continued, however, the more Villa became defensively orientated. The crowd booed at continual back-passing from the visitors and outside-right Jimmy Brown was booked in the final minute for time wasting. But the visitors got what they came for - a point.

> ## – MAN OF THE MATCH –
>
> *DAVID MILLS was singled out by the Villa manager Vic Crowe, who said: "His determined running posed us the biggest threat, while he was unlucky to hit the woodwork."*

David Mills' all action display earned him the Man of the Match Award against Aston Villa.

The dedicated staff of Ayresome Park 1973-74 : Left to right, Mr R. Hunt, Mrs E. Price, Mrs A Burton, Mrs S. Neeve, Mrs M. Black, Mr T.H.C. Green (Club Secretary), Mrs N.Thompson, Mrs N. Postgate, Mr W. Baxter, Mr C. Edon.

– NEWS UPDATE –

Souness praised

BORO were now joint top with Sunderland, Bolton, Bristol City and Villa. Only Sunderland and Villa remained unbeaten, while Cardiff were just one point behind.

Of the Villa game, Charlton said: "We played with control and I enjoyed the game. We were up against six or seven defenders all the time, but we played well and we are beginning to look for the right things, while Souness is settling in nicely."

*   *   *   *   *

Crucial signing

BOBBY Murdoch had a pedigree which was the envy of many within the game. At club level he had done the lot, at international level he had served Scotland well, but, at 29, he was being edged out of the Glasgow Celtic side and had played just 24 games the previous season.

Reserve team football was not befitting such a player. Jock Stein was aware of what Jack Charlton was attempting to build on Teesside. The two managers were good friends and it was that friendship which lead to Murdoch becoming a Middlesbrough player on Monday, September 17. The fee, remarkably, was nothing.

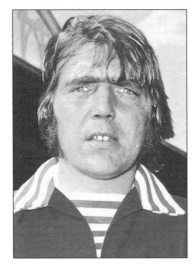

The free transfer signing of the inspirational Bobby Murdoch from Celtic provided Jack Charlton with the missing link that had always eluded Stan Anderson.

"I have been an admirer of Bobby ever since he whacked one past me in the European Cup semi-final in 1970," said Charlton.

"I'm as chuffed as little apples that he has signed for us. I was afraid it would be a free for all when he became available on a free transfer.

"But I have spent a lot of time with Jock Stein since I joined Boro and he telephoned me last week to say he was letting Bobby go. Naturally I asked if I could talk to him before anyone else."

As for Murdoch, he admitted: "This move will put the edge back on my game. Boro are an ambitious club and I'm looking forward to playing on that great pitch.

"I have played on it only once before, when I played for the Scottish League against the English League five years ago.

"I think I can do a good job for this club. I joined Celtic from school and there have been times during my career that I thought I might be missing out on something by not playing in England."

Murdoch travelled with Middlesbrough for their next game, which was on the day he joined. But he took no part in the game at Brisbane Road against Orient.

*   *   *   *   *

MONDAY SEPTEMBER 17
Orient 0   Middlesbrough 0

ORIENT	MIDDLESBROUGH
Goddard	Platt
Payne	Craggs
Downing	Spraggon
Allen	Souness
Hoadley	Boam
Walley	Maddren
Fairbrother	McMordie
Brisley	Mills
Bullock	Hickton
Queen	Foggon
Heppolette	Armstrong
Sub: Fisher	Sub: Smith

Attendance: 9,744.

Match Report

BORO went to the top of the table after this goalless draw in the capital. Despite the lack of goals, it was a highly entertaining affair and a fair result.

Boro created a number of chances, although the closest they came to scoring was when David Armstrong hit the crossbar 30 seconds from the end.

"I'm getting closer," joked Armstrong afterwards. "Last week I shot just over. Maybe I'll score soon."

Armstrong came in for credit from Bobby Murdoch, who was watching in the stands, the 29 year old Scot saying: "I am looking forward to playing in that side. What a prospect that Armstrong is."

Boro had to fight for their share of the spoils. Orient created few chances but always worked hard and it took all of Boro's organising skills to keep their hosts at bay.

Most of the London managers had gone along to watch the game and they were quick to praise Charlton's side, with Jack saying: "Everyone told me what a fine team I had. The way the lads fought did my heart good.

"It's great to be top. It may be for only a short time, but we'll be there battling at the finish."

Orient v Middlesbrough
Monday 17th September

No way through at floodlit Brisbane Road : Above, Frank Spraggon, (No.3), John Craggs and Willie Maddren snuff out an Orient attack, while below, Stuart Boam, (No.5) also displays the defensive organisation which was to characterise the season as he heads clear.

– NEWS UPDATE –

Big Jack comeback

THE first time Bobby Murdoch (right) pulled on a Boro shirt was when playing for the reserves two days after he joined the club.

Jack Charlton also played in the game, which attracted 2,000 fans. Charlton even scored the winner.

He was playing just to get in a bit of match practice ahead of a guest appearance in a testimonial game for Eusebio in Lisbon.

The reason for Murdoch's appearance was given by Charlton, who said: "I just want Bobby to get involved in the club and the best way to do that is to play."

Charlton revealed that Murdoch was in his plans for the forthcoming game at Blackpool.

Bobby Murdoch had his first Boro run out in the reserves with Big Jack.

* * * * *

SATURDAY SEPTEMBER 22

Blackpool 0   Middlesbrough 0

BLACKPOOL	**MIDDLESBROUGH**
Wood	Platt
Halton	Craggs
Bentley	Spraggon
Alcock	Souness
James	Boam
Suddaby	Maddren
Burns	Murdoch
Suddick	Mills
Davies	Hickton
Rafferty	Foggon
Walsh	Armstrong
Sub: Dyson	Sub: Smith

Attendance: 14,784.

Match Report

BOBBY Murdoch's dream of playing in the English League finally arrived on a cool afternoon in Blackpool. Eric McMordie had failed to recover from a slight groin strain suffered against Orient and was left out.

A coach load of Celtic fans, on route to watch Leeds v Manchester United, changed their plans on hearing Murdoch was to play and arrived at Bloomfield Road to swell the number of Boro supporters.

Boro had been knocked off the top

Blackpool forward, Mickey Burns, a recruit to Ayresome Park in the 1970s, was a constant threat during Boro's hard-earned draw at Bloomfield Road.

of the table in the week leading up to the game after Villa's 1-1 home draw with Fulham.

Blackpool included former Newcastle player Alan Suddick. He returned after missing the previous three games with a groin strain.

Micky Walsh was moved to the left wing in place of Kevin Tully in a Blackpool side which had beaten Crystal Palace on the Monday.

Murdoch was almost prominent, but Blackpool did much of the pressing with Micky Burns and Alan Suddick ever prominent. Walsh was also a constant threat to the Boro on the left flank.

Blackpool looked the more likely winners, but Boro stuck to their guns by giving nothing away, and it was a well earned point at the final whistle.

– MAN OF THE MATCH –

THE Blackpool manager Harry Potts couldn't split Boro's defensive duo of STUART BOAM and WILLIE MADDREN. He explained his choice by saying: "They had the most to do. They were under the most pressure and did very well. They worked well together."

– NEWS UPDATE –

Dull display

BOBBY Murdoch's reaction to his first game south of the border was simple: "I felt quite good and was happy to feel so strong at the end, but the English game seems a wee bit quick."

As for the club's reaction, that came from coach Ian MacFarlane (right) who said: "That was our dullest display away from home this season, but the result was right."

Ian MacFarlane

*   *   *   *   *

Platt call-up

CHARLTON flew out to Lisbon on the Monday after the Blackpool game, saying he felt guilty at leaving the team behind.

There was another absentee from the training field as goalkeeper Jim Platt joined the Northern Ireland squad for a World Cup game against Bulgaria.

The conflict in the province meant that no games could be played there and this game was to be played at Hillsborough.

Platt was called in as cover as Pat Jennings had withdrawn injured and Willie MacFaul had stepped up to the first team.

Both were back in the Boro camp in time to prepare for the game against a Bristol City side which had not won at Ayresome Park since the Second World War. In fact City had lost six on the trot on Teesside and had drawn only three of their last 13 visits. However, they were unbeaten away from home this season, taking five out of a possible six points.

City included 6'2" centre-half David Rodgers despite having a broken nose, but there was a doubt about leading scorer Bobby Gould, who hadn't trained all week because of a hamstring strain.

*   *   *   *   *

Match Report

BOBBY Murdoch's home debut proved to be a winning one. Not only that, a goalscoring one as well.

Bristol City suffered their first away defeat of the season as Boro swept to the top of the First Division. This time there would be no knocking them off. Boro were to stay top of the tree for the remainder of the season.

A win over the Robins looked unlikely in a sluggish, scrappy first half. Boro gave the ball away a lot and looked a shade anxious.

The second half saw a different Boro. Charlton's side completely dominated affairs.

Looking more relaxed, Boro knocked the ball around well and ripped City's defence open time and time again. But it took a spectacular effort to open the scoring.

A well worked move was rounded off by Murdoch who hammered an unstoppable 25 yard drive beyond the City 'keeper on the hour.

"I just happened to be on the spot for a rehearsed move," said Murdoch after the game.

"It could have been anyone else there for the final shot. I was quite pleased with my home debut, although I felt my passing wasn't up to standard. But the lads are all working for each other and that's what it's all about."

Boro had to wait until six minutes from time before doubling their advantage, David Armstrong cutting through the visitors' defence to hammer a low drive in off the far post to become the seventh different Boro player to score so far that season.

"We're getting better," enthused Charlton afterwards.

"We're using the park as we've never used it before. Murdoch lacks a bit of pace, but he is such a good user of the ball and can bring players into the game when you never expect it. It's great to be back top, now we have to stay there."

SATURDAY SEPTEMBER 29
Middlesbrough 2   Bristol City 0

MIDDLESBROUGH	BRISTOL CITY
Platt	Cashley
Craggs	Sweeney
Spraggon	Drysdale
Souness	Emanuel
Boam	Rodgers
Maddren	Merrick
Murdoch	Tainton
Mills	Ritchie (Gillies 72)
Hickton	Gould
Foggon	Gow
Armstrong	Fear
Sub: Charlton	

Scorers: Murdoch 60, Armstrong 84.

Attendance: 17,069.

– MAN OF THE MATCH –

JOHN CRAGGS was the nomination of the Bristol City manager Alan Dicks, brother of former Boro full-back Ronnie. Alan said: " Although Craggs made a number of mistakes, especially in the first half, he always wanted to be involved.

"That was the main difference between him and some of my players. He played some excellent football at times."

Middlesbrough v Bristol City
Saturday 29th September

What a home debut: Bobby Murdoch, right, celebrates his first goal for the Boro against Bristol City.

Second Division League Table - 28-9-73

	P	W	D	L	F	A	Pts
Bristol City	7	5	1	1	10	5	11
Aston Villa	7	2	5	0	4	4	9
Nottingham Forest	7	3	3	1	12	6	9
Fulham	7	3	3	1	6	4	9
MIDDLESBROUGH	**7**	**3**	**3**	**1**	**5**	**4**	**9**
Orient	7	2	4	1	10	7	8

REFLECTIONS

John Craggs

YOU wouldn't think so by his style of play, but the instruction to John Craggs was to defend first and if there was a chance to move forward, do so. But only if there was no danger left behind.

Craggs was one of the best exponents of the attacking full-back role in the game at the time and his philosophy was simple.

"Wingers were great when they were running at you, but they weren't so keen to run backwards!"

It was a philosophy which worked to great effect. Time and again surging runs would have the opposition left-back called into play sooner than he had expected as Boro's right-back entered his territory in double quick time.

John could defend, very effectively, but always chose to attack whenever he could.

" My thinking was, of course, to keep an eye on the winger, but once you had him turning, on the run away from your goal, you always had a chance to get the ball into the box.

"The system Jack played was simple. One at the front post, one at the back, so when you delivered your cross into the box it wasn't just hit and hope."

It was the simplicity of play which took Boro to heights which had hitherto been unthought of.

"Football is a simple game, it's the players who make it difficult," reasons Craggs. "When a player starts trying to do fancy things on the ball in the wrong area, that's when there is a problem.

"We never had that. We were always told to keep it simple, to pass to a man in a red shirt, and keep the ball with your team. It was simple as that. We weren't doing anything different, just better than the rest."

Craggs admits he didn't know what to expect when Jack Charlton took over. Stan Anderson had been a fixture before getting the sack in the January of that year, while Harold Sheperdson had taken over until the summer, when in walked Big Jack.

"We knew about him, but we didn't know what to expect. But what he brought was organisation and a blend which worked. Obviously he had come from a successful club at Leeds where everyone had their responsibilities from the tea-boy to Don Revie and his famous dossiers about other teams.

"We were all given a role in the team, a responsibility and if you were doing what you were told, or at least be seen to be doing as you were told, then everything was all right with Jack.

"If you started to step out of line then he would have a

word. If you did it again you were out of the team. We didn't have too many changes that season!"

In terms of 'doing as you were told', the players were briefed on the opposition in the week leading up to every game but, if at all possible, they tried to impose their way of playing on their opponents.

"There were obviously tricky opponents, but with due respect, it wasn't until we went into the First Division that I had a really tricky winger to mark. Gordon Hill of Millwall was the best in the Second Division, and he later went on to Manchester United, while I played against Peter Thompson when he had just signed for Bolton.

"I had played against him when he was with Liverpool and I was with Newcastle. He was a handful at times. He would just run straight at you. He wouldn't beat you with any tricky footwork, just sheer pace, and he was quick, believe me.

"In the First Division the most difficult player I came across was Steve Heighway of Liverpool. He was a right handful. But the lads in the Second Division were not that good, and didn't hold any fears for us."

CHAPTER FIVE

OCTOBER

Early consolidation

BORO'S next game came just three days later, an early conclusion to their meetings with Orient.

The London side had travelled north on the Monday, staying in Saltburn, and had prepared themselves with a work out on the coast road between Marske and Redcar.

Unbeaten in four games away from home, Orient would go top of the table if they won.

They named the same side which had played Swindon on the Saturday, while Boro were unchanged from the team which beat Bristol City.

*   *   *   *   *

TUESDAY OCTOBER 2

Middlesbrough 3   Orient 2

MIDDLESBROUGH	ORIENT
Platt	Goddard
Craggs	Payne
Spraggon	Downing
Souness	Allen
Boam	Hoadley
Maddren	Walley
Murdoch	Fairbrother
Mills (Charlton 61)	Brisley (Linton)
Hickton	Bullock
Foggon	Queen
Armstrong	Heppolette

Scorers: Foggon 24, Hickton pen 77, Bullock 78, Heppolette 81, Hickton 84.

Attendance: 22,164.

– MAN OF THE MATCH –

"ANY one of your ten defenders,"was the sarcastic reply from a normally friendly and amiable George Petchey. "But if I had to single one out it would be STUART BOAM. He won a lot of balls in the air and was the strongest defender."

Match Report

TWO sides who were clearly among the best in the division in the early part of the season fought out a really tough uncompromising encounter.

Alan Foggon headed home a David Armstrong cross to give Boro the lead after 24 minutes, but they had to defend for long spells afterwards.

Orient couldn't find a way through and Boro turned the tables, applying pressure of their own.

David Mills, who had been injured as early as the sixth minute, limped off with knee ligament damage shortly after the hour, but it was Boro who scored next amidst a sea of controversy.

Left-half Tom Walley was adjudged to have handled the ball inside the area and John Hickton rattled home the penalty.

Orient, incensed by the decision, pulled one back a minute later when Micky Bullock blasted home a fierce shot. Three minutes later the visitors were level when Ricky Heppolette gave Jim Platt no chance with a header.

Six minutes from time a superb cross from substitute Harry Charlton was headed home by Hickton for his second of the game and Boro's winner.

"It was never a penalty," blasted Orient boss George Petchey afterwards.

"I had a word with the linesman and he said he didn't give it, the ref did. The ball hit the player high up the arm. He never handled it."

Derrick Downing

Former Boro player Derrick Downing (left) agreed, saying: "It was nothing like a penalty, but at least it motivated us. We were really mad with the decision."

Orient found an unlikely ally in the shape of John Hickton who said: "I didn't think it was a penalty and I didn't want to take it after I missed against Carlisle.

" I was terrified! I asked if anyone else wanted to take it, but Boamy said I had to."

As for Charlton, he had mixed feelings: "I wouldn't like to say if it was a penalty or not, but what I do know is that I would like to think my players would fight like that if they went two goals down.

" The crowd were great. It has been a fight to get them here and our next target has to be 30,000."

Songbirds

BORO'S players almost became involved in a row with a local school about the club's first official song.

Two major record companies were interested in a song done by Staplyton School in Eston. However Boro's players wanted to do a song of their own.

Initially the children sang a song called "Boro are a great club" for the players to record later.

But after an airing on BBC Radio Teesside (now Radio Cleveland) and at Ayresome Park, the response from the public was tremendous.

BBC Radio Teesside's music producer said: "It is an interesting problem. But the old showbiz maxim of children singing always sells records is a powerful one. We will have to have an audition for the players and let the public choose."

The school was initially asked to sing six songs in a Radio Teesside competition, but music master Terry Parker wrote an extra song for the 15 strong choir whose ages ranged from 11-13, and they walked away with the competition.

The potential problem was resolved when an agreement was reached which saw the players and children work together on a record which was put together after 30 takes!

* * * * *

Introducing
The Boro Choral Society

Hitting the high notes with gusto: The "Boro Choral Society" and the children of Staplyton School, Eston, recording the new club song.

– NEWS UPDATE –

Recognition for Charlton

BY way of recognition for Boro's fine start to the season, Jack Charlton was named Manager Of The Month for September.

Charlton won a gallon bottle of Bell's Scotch Whisky and a cheque for £100.

Other divisional awards were: First Division, Gordon Milne (Coventry City); Third Division, Don Megson (Bristol Rovers); Fourth Division, Charlie Hurley (Reading).

"It's a nice award for the lads," said Charlton.

"You can't win these awards on your own, without them you win nothing. The big prize for me is at the end of the season."

*   *   *   *   *

Mills bomb

BORO were rocked with the news that they would have to do without David Mills for the forthcoming games against Swindon at the County Ground and Manchester United in the League Cup.

Mills had damaged knee ligaments against Orient and was ordered to rest.

"It's terrible to be out of the team when they are starting to do so well," said Mills.

"But my leg is very sore and there is no way I can play at the moment. I just hope I won't be out for too long."

*   *   *   *   *

Jack Charlton accepting a Manager of the Month Award. This was to be one of the many accolades both he and his team would receive during the momentous 1973/74 season.

39

– NEWS UPDATE –

Soaked in Swindon

MALCOLM Smith was the player to take over from David Mills.

The 20 year old striker from Ferryhill had played for the reserves in midweek, as had Bill Gates, who was named as a sub.

The game was played in pouring rain on a greasy surface, while the pre-match entertainment came from an evangelist!

*   *   *   *   *

SATURDAY OCTOBER 6

Swindon Town 0   Middlesbrough 1

SWINDON TOWN	**MIDDLESBROUGH**
Allan	Platt
Thomas	Craggs
Trollope	Spraggon
Butler	Souness
Burrows	Boam
Potter (Syrett 75)	Maddren
Moss	Murdoch
Bunkell	Smith
Collins	Hickton
Treacy	Foggon
Jenkins	Armstrong
	Sub: Gates

Scorer: Murdoch 72.

Attendance: 6,787.

Match Report

DOUBTLESS taking heart from the evangelist, Boro moved straight on to the attack with David Armstrong shooting just wide.

But it was Swindon who could have taken the lead, centre-forward Peter Collins hitting the side netting when he should have scored from close range.

Boro's defence had to mass ranks to clear after Jim Platt dropped a header from Ray Treacy. However, while Swindon were playing well enough, it was Boro who looked more dangerous and Hickton had a goal disallowed for pushing.

It was a game which contained a lot of effort, but the conditions were such that good football was at a premium.

Malcolm Smith missed a sitter ten minutes into the second half, spooning over from almost under the crossbar, and it was left to Bobby Murdoch to produce the match winner in the 72nd minute.

Alan Foggon was tackled from behind and looked to be in a lot of pain, but the referee played advantage. Boro broke, sweeping into attack and David Armstrong sent over a perfect cross with Murdoch arriving late and hammering a first time shot into the net.

In the closing stages Treacy shot just over for Swindon, as did Murdoch and Boam for Boro.

There was a row after the game with the Swindon manager Les Allen claiming Boro's goal was offside.

"Foggon was running like a stag when he was brought down. How could he be offside when he had taken the ball with him? It was good goal and we deserved to win," was the emphatic judgement of Jack Charlton.

– MAN OF THE MATCH –

JOHN HICKTON was the one singled out by Les Allen, the Swindon manager. His reason? "He was always there when Boro wanted to clear and that took a lot of pressure off the defence. He did a very good job for his team." Hickton's response: "I thought it was one of my poorest games of the season!"

A typically towering header from Boro captain Stuart Boam, (No 5), ensured another clean sheet at the County Ground, Swindon.

– NEWS UPDATE –

Magnificent in Manchester

BORO'S first game in the League Cup that season was at Old Trafford.

Manchester United were struggling and Boro were in confident mood going over the Pennines.

They were not concerned that the game came just two days after their win at Swindon.

United were struggling in sixth bottom position in the First Division and were to be relegated at the end of the season.

At the time they played Boro they had taken just eight points from ten games.

Manager Tommy Docherty dropped Irish international Sammy McIlroy for the game. McIlroy had replaced Trevor Anderson after he was injured 15 minutes into the 2-1 defeat at Wolves on Saturday.

Despite the fact that McIlroy had gone on to score, he was left out of the side to face Boro as Eire international Gerry Daly was recalled.

Boro named the same team which won at Swindon.

*   *   *   *   *

MONDAY OCTOBER 8

Manchester United 0   Middlesbrough 1

MANCHESTER UNITED	MIDDLESBROUGH
Stepney	Platt
M Buchan	Craggs
Young	Spraggon
Greenhoff	Souness
Holton	Boam
James	Maddren
Morgan	Murdoch
Daly	Smith
Kidd	Hickton
Macari	Foggon
Graham	Armstrong
Sub: G Buchan	Sub: Gates

Scorer: Smith 3.

Attendance: 23,906.

Manchester United manager Tommy Docherty praised John Hickton's performance when the Boro recorded a famous 1-0 victory at Old Trafford in the League Cup.

Match Report

BORO'S league form followed them into the cup.

After scoring early in the game they defended doggedly against a side who were off form in the league, but one which still had enough quality to make Boro suffer.

But, just as Boro's league form had stayed with them, so did United's and Boro recorded a famous victory.

Malcolm Smith opened the scoring after just three minutes. Alan Foggon, playing despite suffering with a sore knee picked up at Swindon, set the ball rolling to Graeme Souness, whose great pass split the United defence apart and Smith capitalised.

"That was the best moment I have ever had in football," said Smith. "I thought a defender would come back with me, but we seemed to catch them by surprise."

United almost equalised in the middle of pressure which was applied for most of the remaining 87 minutes after Boro scored.

Tony Young saw a close range effort rebound off a post and into the hands of a grateful Jim Platt.

"I didn't see the ball coming through a crowd of players," said Platt, " I was lucky that it hit a post and I was able to smother it as Gerry Daly came in.

"Someone whacked me in the head and it hurt for the rest of the game, but it doesn't matter."

Boro were never overawed. Extremely well organised, they were often booed for time wasting, while Smith and John Hickton ran themselves into the ground when given a chance to chase a clearance.

Souness played what was described as "his best game to date" while Boro's captain Stuart Boam had not lost sight of what really mattered that season, promotion.

"The win over United was our best away performance of the season, but the result of the night was Sunderland's 2-2 draw at Derby.

"It means with their European commitments (Sunderland had won the FA Cup the previous season) and the replay, they are building up a back-log of fixtures.

"They are promotion candidates along with ourselves and it's the league which counts."

The win for Boro increased the pressure on a club who were struggling. United's directors had to face shareholders the next day to explain a loss of £390,469 for the past year.

Manager Tommy Docherty was facing another problem off the pitch as Lou Macari was unsettled. Docherty outlined the position when saying: "Macari refused to play for the second team and refused to come into the club to discuss the situation.

"So I went to see him, fined him and placed him on the transfer list. As a club we have struggled, but our youth policy has been put on a better footing and our second team is top of the Central League. We are getting geared for success and feel we are improving."

– MAN OF THE MATCH –

UNITED manager Tommy Docherty picked JOHN HICKTON.
"I have always admired Hickton as a player. He did a tremendous amount of running and work for his side."

– NEWS UPDATE –

Press reaction

THE local and national press were certainly impressed by what they had seen of Middlesbrough and Tuesday's papers were full of it.

DAILY MIRROR: There was only one team of First Division quality out there and it wasn't Manchester United.

DAILY MAIL: Boro covered themselves in glory when they swept Manchester United off the League Cup trail. The Second Division leaders outclassed and outpaced the First Division side.

YORKSHIRE POST: The goal was laced with the many qualities which gave Middlesbrough a distinct edge. Speed of thought, speed off the mark and an eye for the straightforward. They were simply superb, superbly simple.

THE GUARDIAN: Jack Charlton has done well with Boro. They are well above the average in most of the essentials, although it would be good to see them play against really strong opposition before making a rash forecast about their chances of winning a trophy this season.

DAILY EXPRESS: Bold and brash Boro added a new dimension to their promotion push, storming through to the third round.

NORTHERN ECHO: Boro fully deserved this triumph. They played better as a team, produced the more skilful football and displayed a confidence which augers well for what should be an exciting season.

DAILY TELEGRAPH: A young well organised team who have prospered under Jack Charlton.

Boro were good value for their victory. They ran, chased and worked tirelessly, giving every ounce of effort.

Boro's 'reward' for their win was an away tie with First Division Stoke City in round three.

* * * * *

Tiger taming

ALL which concerned Boro's management was the Saturday game at home to Hull.

The glory of the win at Old Trafford washed over Charlton, who was in no mood to get carried away with anything.

Boro were forced to make a change on the morning of the game as Harry Charlton, who was to take over the role of substitute from Bill Gates, went down with a stomach upset and his place was taken by Malcolm Poskett.

A South Bank lad, Poskett had never played for the first team before, although he was scoring freely for the reserves.

He, together with Harry Charlton and Frank McGivern, 2, had scored for the reserves in a 4-0 win away to Scunthorpe Reserves at the Old Show Ground on a windswept night during the week.

Hull City manager Terry Neill had defensive problems. Malcolm Lord was injured and Jimmy McGill was starting a suspension, having been sent off at Cardiff two weeks earlier. So Roger de Vries had to play despite being doubtful all week.

The Tigers had drawn 3-3 with Leicester City in a midweek League Cuptie.

Jack Charlton was presented with his Manager Of The Month award for September before the kick-off.

* * * * *

Malcolm Poskett made his only Boro first team appearance when he played the last 12 minutes against Hull City at Ayresome Park.

SATURDAY OCTOBER 13

Middlesbrough 1	Hull City 0
MIDDLESBROUGH	**HULL CITY**
Platt	Wealands
Craggs	Banks
Spraggon	Vries
Souness	Kaye (O'Riley 11)
Boam	Deere
Maddren	Blampey
Murdoch	Hawley
Smith (Poskett 78)	Galvin
Hickton	Pearson
Foggon	Wagstaff
Armstrong	Greenwood

Scorer: Smith 47.

Attendance: 22,135.

Match Report

BORO increased their lead at the top of the table to three points with this hard fought win.

They almost scored after two minutes, Alan Foggon sending Malcolm Smith through, with the youngster denied by ex-Darlington goalkeper Jeff Wealands.

Experienced wing-half John Kaye was carried off following a challenge by John Craggs with only seven minutes gone and that seemed to unsettle the visitors.

Wealands earned his corn in the City goal as Boro piled on the pressure, but they were left exposed at times as Hull broke quickly.

On one such raid Jim Platt acrobatically tipped over a powerful shot from Stuart Pearson.

Boro's winner came two minutes into the second half. John Craggs played a good ball through to Alan Foggon and he switched it inside to Smith, who scored with a cool back-heeled flick which went in, just inside the post.

Boro appealed that a header from Stuart Boam had crossed the line later in the game, while Smith missed a sitter. He was taken off with 12 minutes remaining, allowing Malcom Poskett his one and only taste of first team football with Boro.

John Hickton, (No 9), displays his poacher's instinct by checking that Malcolm Smith's shot had crossed the line for the winning goal against Hull City.

– NEWS UPDATE –

World Cup misery

DISMAY had taken hold of English football by the time Boro next took to the field.

The national team had failed to beat Poland at Wembley the previous Wednesday and therefore failed to qualify for the World Cup Finals in Munich.

That, coupled with driving rain, had an affect on the attendance for the game against West Brom.

The Baggies had been relegated from the First Division the previous season and were making their first visit to Ayresome Park since 1954. They had drawn 1-1 with Carlisle the previous Saturday and had no injury worries.

David Mills passed a fitness test on the morning of the game and returned for Boro ahead of Malcolm Smith, with Charlton explaining the change saying: "Malcolm has done extremely well, but Mills is the No.1 in that position and he plays."

* * * * *

SATURDAY OCTOBER 20

Middlesbrough 0	West Brom 0

MIDDLESBROUGH	**WEST BROM**
Platt	Latchford
Craggs	Nisbet
Spraggon	Merrick
Souness	Cantello
Boam	Wile
Maddren	Robertson
Murdoch	Hartford
Mills	T Brown
Hickton (Smith 73)	A Brown
Foggon	Shaw
Armstrong	Johnston
	Sub: Glover

Attendance: 18,997.

Match Report

THE conditions played a major part in this goalless draw, although both sides gave it their best shot.

Boro started brightly, creating two early chances, the best of which fell to David Mills. But he hit the side netting instead of the back of the net.

It wasn't a day to be a goalkeeper and Albion, breaking free from Boro pressure, almost scored when Jim Platt dropped a low drive at the feet of Alistair Brown, before finally gathering at the second attempt.

Mills and Hickton fired in shots which went just wide, while a dreadful backpass from Bobby Murdoch, who had a poor game, was intercepted by Tony Brown, who shot wide.

Alan Foggon had a 'goal' disallowed, while John Craggs brought a brilliant save out of Peter Latchford. Willie Johnston was just wide for the Baggies, Graeme Souness likewise for Boro, while David Armstrong missed when he should have scored.

Albion almost stole it late in the game, but Tony Brown rattled a Willie Johnston cross against the bar.

– MAN OF THE MATCH –

THE West Brom manager Don Howe singled out DAVID MILLS for the award. He said: "Mills was up and down that wing all the time and it struck me that if anyone was going to break us down it would be him."

John Hickton, centre, outjumps the West Brom defence at Ayresome Park. But the determined Baggies eventually held out for a share of the spoils.

– NEWS UPDATE –

Souness stupidity

BORO'S so called defensive tactics were the topic for discussion prior to the game against Carlisle on the Tuesday after the Albion game.

Charlton, defending the way his side played the game, said: "I'm not going to change my tactics. I'm not going to put four up front and start giving lots of goals away.

"Our formation suits the players we have. Our defence has played well, but we are not defensive. We are creating plenty of chances, but the hardest thing in the game is putting the ball in the back of the net and I have to say our finishing leaves a lot to be desired."

Charlton found an ally in Carlisle manager Alan Ashman. "We in the game all laugh at these outbursts about defensive soccer.

"Everyone knows that all successful sides are first based on strong defences. Boro have been taking some stick for their lack of goals, but they are top of the table and therefore the best side."

Carlisle had won 1-0 at Crystal Palace (struggling at the bottom of the table) on Saturday and kept the same team. It was a team which did not include bargain buy from Walsall, Ray Train, who was still missing with a knee injury.

Included in the side was John Gorman, later to achieve fame on the international stage with Glenn Hoddle and England, as well as domestic roles with Swindon and Ipswich.

*   *   *   *   *

TUESDAY OCTOBER 23

Carlisle United 1   Middlesbrough 1

CARLISLE UNITED	MIDDLESBROUGH
Ross	Platt
Carr	Craggs
Gorman	Spraggon
O'Neill	Souness
Green	Boam
Tiler	Maddren
Martin	Murdoch
Ternant	Mills
Owen	Hickton
Clarke	Foggon
Laidlaw	Armstrong
	Sub: Smith

Scorers: Foggon 3, Martin 80.

Attendance: 11,152.

– MAN OF THE MATCH –

CARLISLE manager Alan Ashman said: "I thought Boro's two best players were Platt and Boam. Boro had a lot of defending to do and the 'keeper stood out."
So PLATT it was who was given the nomination.

Match Report

CARLISLE had made a relatively poor start to the season, but had picked up in recent weeks, taking nine points from the last 12 on offer and were lying in 12th place with 12 points.

Boro rattled the home side almost immediately, taking the lead after just two minutes with a cracking goal from Alan Foggon.

But if Boro thought they were in for an easy ride they had to think again.

Carlisle dominated for long periods and Boro's case wasn't helped when Graeme Souness was sent-off just before half-time.

"As I moved past Stan Ternant, who was on the floor, he kicked me, not once, but twice " was the explanation of Souness, who carried on: "So I clipped him. Not hard, but I clipped him and I'm now as sick as a parrot. Things were going so well for me this season."

Souness gained no sympathy from his manager in the dressing room afterwards, with Charlton saying: "I accept players playing hard, but I don't accept those who go over the top, or those who strike an opponent.

"If he does it again he will be fined by the club. I have no complaints about the decision. You cannot use your hands in this game."

Boro's task was made harder with the dismissal of Souness and they started to play possession football, which annoyed the home fans.

Back passing continually frustrated the home side until the 80th minute when a shot from Martin took a deflection off Stuart Boam and Jim Platt was left helpless as Carlisle drew level.

Boro took a point from the game, but Souness also took a three match ban away from Brunton Park.

A fine display of goalkeeping by Jim Platt, ensured the Boro gained a hard-earned point at Carlisle United.

– NEWS UPDATE –

Into the Lions' den

PRIOR to the game with Millwall, Boro's forwards were given specialist training with the emphasis on one-on-one and two-on-one. They were told to be more positive.

John Hickton was taken into hospital to have fluid removed from a knee and missed his first game of the season.

Eric McMordie was called into the squad for the first time since the middle of September and Tony McAndrew for the first time ever, but it was Malcolm Smith who was chosen to replace Hickton.

Teenager Tony McAndrew, who had first come to the notice of the Boro fans when he was sent-off in a pre-season reserve game at Whitby, for swearing at the referee, was named as sub.

Millwall went into the game on the back of three straight wins, a run which followed a sequence of five straight defeats.

Millwall manager Benny Fenton said: "There will be a lot of stick flying about and we won't be knocked about in this one.

"We want to play entertaining football, but if Boro want to play it hard then we will too."

Boro captain, Stuart Boam retorted: "They may be over confident. If we can draw at Carlisle with ten men we can do well at Millwall, I'm sure."

* * * * *

SATURDAY OCTOBER 27
Millwall 0   Middlesbrough 1

MILLWALL	**MIDDLESBROUGH**
King	Platt
Donaldson	Craggs
Jones	Spraggon
Dorney	Souness
Kitchener	Boam
Burnett	Maddren
Brown	Murdoch
Clark	Mills
Wood	Smith
Dunphy (Bolland 70)	Foggon
Hill	Armstrong
	Sub: McAndrew

Scorer: Smith 44.   Attendance: 13,253.

The robust Millwall forward, Alf Wood, was later signed by Jack Charlton in October 1976.

Match Report

FOR all the fighting talk, Jack Charlton received a standing ovation from the Millwall fans at The Den as he took his place in the dug-out.

The early exchanges produced an open game, Alan Dorney heading an Alan Foggon cross clear. David Armstrong and Graeme Souness combined to give Malcolm Smith a difficult chance, while Frank Spraggon had to be smart at the back as the home side pressed.

Bobby Murdoch, back on form, teased and tormented in equal measure, while Alf Wood, later to play for Boro and who had scored a hat-trick in a 5-1 win over Preston in his previous game, was inches over for the home side.

Barry Kitchener appeared to elbow David Mills, but this proved to be an isolated incident in an otherwise keenly fought, but clean game.

Boro's match winner came against the run of play, a minute from half-time. John Craggs burst through on the right and crossed to Foggon, who helped the ball into the goalmouth where Malcolm Smith, arriving late, blasted past Bryan King.

Millwall hit back at the start of the second half and Jim Platt had to be alert to tip over a dipping header from Wood, while Eamon Dunphy shot just wide and the Lions had penalty appeals turned down.

Winger Gordon Hill almost equalised 15 minutes from time, Platt again coming to the rescue when tipping over the bar. Hill also hit the bar in the closing stages.

Platt admitted: "I was lucky, I should have got a better touch to the ball. It hit the bar and could have gone anywhere. If it had hit me on the back of the head it would have gone in."

Close to time Millwall claimed a close range effort had gone over the line, but the referee was having none of it.

"We got a break and made the most of it," was the honest assessment of Jack Charlton, while Malcolm Smith was critical of his own performance, saying: "I'm not happy with my game. I'm looking for something a lot more, especially in control."

Equally critical, but of Middlesbrough, was the Millwall manager Benny Fenton, who said: "They had one shot and scored. They employed two up front and nine at the back. By contrast we entertained the public with our two orthodox wingers. We played attractive and skilful football which should have brought goals.

"It's not sour grapes. They are top of the table and I wish we were, good luck to Middlesbrough and Jack Charlton."

– MAN OF THE MATCH –

BENNY Fenton refused to nominate a Middlesbrough player, so the nomination was left to an experienced London journalist, Colin Cameron.
"BOBBY MURDOCH had a tremendous game. All the London press were talking about his talent."

Cup of cheer

BORO'S next fixture took them to the Potteries and a League Cup third round tie at First Division Stoke City.

The home side were in good heart for the game at the Victoria Ground, having beaten Coventry City by 3-0 the previous Saturday.

However, they had picked up three injuries during that game. Defender Denis Smith, midfield player John Mahoney (later to join Boro) and striker John Ritchie were all passed fit to play, although Stoke were without veteran midfield player George Eastham and winger Terry Conroy, who both were waiting for cartilage operations.

Jimmy Greenhoff, who played alongside Charlton at Leeds, was in the Stoke side, along with Geoff Hurst.

Boro went into the game without a recognised first choice striker as John Hickton was still suffering from a knee injury and David Mills had been up all night suffering with a stomach upset.

This gave a chance to a 20 year old London boy Peter Brine. His father, a Scarborough postman, had written to Boro asking for a trial for his 15 year old son.

Brine Junior had scored 67 goals for London junior side Winns Wanderers before joining Boro as an apprentice. He had made his league debut in January 1973 in a goalless draw at home to QPR, after which Stan Anderson resigned.

This season Brine had previously been substitute against Crystal Palace and Aston Villa.

Youngster Tony McAndrew was named as substitute.

The last time Boro had played Stoke was in a Second Division game in the 1962-63 season when Stanley Matthews was playing.

* * * * *

World Cup hat-trick hero Geoff Hurst failed to make the scoresheet as Boro gained a very creditable 1-1 draw against First Division Stoke City in the League Cup.

WEDNESDAY OCTOBER 31

Stoke City 1   Middlesbrough 1

STOKE CITY	MIDDLESBROUGH
Farmer	Platt
Marsh	Craggs
Pejic	Spraggon
Mahoney	Souness
Smith	Boam
Dodd	Maddren
Robertson	Murdoch
Greenhoff	Smith
Ritchie	Brine
Hurst	Foggon
Haselgrave	Armstrong
Sub: Goodwin	Sub: McAndrew

Scorers: Pejic 50, Brine 55.

Attendance: 19,194.

Match Report

BORO were drawn away in each round of the cups that season and, having won at Manchester United, were in good heart for another crack at a First Division side.

They had to fight for everything at the Victoria Ground in a game which was arguably harder than that at Old Trafford.

There were not that many chances in the match overall. Boro, without a recognised first team striker, had to defend for long spells, but were not defensive in their approach, attacking with pace on the break.

In a game as tight as this was, a slip is often the difference between the two sides and that was the way of things on this occasion, or so many thought, after Mike Pejic put Stoke into the lead five minutes into the second half following a John Craggs mistake.

It took Boro just five minutes to equalise. A Bobby Murdoch throw-in was delivered into the box by David Armstrong and Peter Brine scored with a low drive.

"I was amazed at the character of the lads," said Charlton. "They never gave an inch and fought for every ball. They got their just reward for all out effort and the people of Teesside should be proud of them.

"Smith and Brine ran themselves into the ground and with lads of this character the future of this club must be good."

– MAN OF THE MATCH –

"JACK CHARLTON," was the nomination of the Stoke boss Tony Waddington.
"I know he wasn't on the pitch, but his know-how has rubbed off.
"If it can't go to Jack, then the award will have to be split among all 11 members of the team. I can't split them. They played brilliantly against the odds."
If Boro were to beat Stoke in the replay, they would be away again to the winners of the replay between Bristol City and Coventry.

REFLECTIONS

Frank Spraggon

AT 28, Frank Spraggon was one of the oldest members of the team when the season started.

He and Bill Gates were the longest serving players, but whereas Gates hung up his boots at the end of the campaign and concentrated on running a sports shop, Spraggon was to miss just three games in league and cup all season.

"You didn't think about the number of games you had to play in those days," says a player who made the left-back spot his own.

"You just got on with it and besides, I was playing in a very good team. I don't think any of us realised just how good it was at the time and I don't think any of us made the best of it.

" We had been close a few times. We'd never been far away, but Jack brought a system with him which worked a treat."

Spraggon won't forget the first words spoken to him by his new manager.

"Jack was fair. By way of introducing himself he put a spread on for the lads, a nice buffet and we thought he was OK. Mind you it was the only buffet he ever put on!

"He spoke to players in turn and said to me, 'at this club there are some good players, some bad players and some moderate players, and you're one of them!'

"I wasn't a good player, I'll admit that, but I could defend. And I fitted into his system. But there was a few glances from the lads when he told me that, but there was no malice with him.

"What he brought to us was organisation, he got players to play. At half time in matches, Jack would go to certain players and say ' if you do this, or do that, this will happen', and it did. He could see things differently.

"I remember one game we played at Burnley in the first season back in the First Division. A lad called Noble was running the show and we were getting run ragged. At half time Jack said to Graeme Souness 'I want you to bury him, the first chance you get just bury him.'

"The first challenge of the second half Graeme went in for a 50-50, straight through ball and player and we were fine after that. We got a 1-1 draw!"

"He got players to play in a system which worked. John Craggs and I used to work well together. He was good at getting forward, I was good at defending the line.

"But a lot of credit has to go to Stan Anderson you know, he put most of that side together."

Anderson was the first former Boro player to manage the team, but he had left in the January and later took up a position with AEK in Athens, only to leave in the following summer.

Spraggon had played left-half in the Anderson days, but had dropped back to play in the role vacated by Gordon Jones and the first season under Charlton was only his second at left-back.

Charlton was playing with a re-organised defence in more ways than one. Brian Taylor had started the season as first choice centre-half with Willie Maddren in midfield.

"Jack always said that Wilbur, as we used to call Willie, was wasted at the back.

"He felt he could do good things in midfield, but moved him back when Brian got injured early in the season.

"Jack never used to like to make too many changes and Willie's knees could have been a problem if he had played all season in midfield."

It wasn't an injury, rather an illness, which saw Spraggon miss his first game of that season, a 2-2 draw at Sheffield Wednesday.

"I had passed blood the night before and I panicked. I was taken to North Ormesby Hospital, but thankfully it was nothing serious. One of the other games I missed was the one when we won the Championship at Luton.

"After playing just about all season, I would have to miss that! I was suffering with 'flu and couldn't even get out of bed. But we'd done the hard work by then! "

Spraggon was part of a defence which set a record for the number of goals conceded in a season, just 30.

"We were supposed to be defensive, but what we had was a good defence and there was a difference. We also scored a few that season, including four at Fulham.

"That night was special. It followed on from a win at West Brom the previous Saturday. All the London press were there for Bobby Moore's debut. Alan Mullery was playing and we murdered them. Boamy scored, so Willie had to. They would compete with each other.

"That had to be the highlight of the season, although I enjoyed THE goal I scored."

Frank's first goal for almost two years and his last for the club came against Millwall.

"I remember a ball coming across the area, John Hickton pushed their lad out of the way and I was a yard out. I put it in but I couldn't believe it had been allowed to stand. There was hell on. Millwall was in the heart of the docklands area at the time. They had some big lads and it was fun and games for a while.

"But that season it didn't matter who we played. We weren't afraid of anybody."

CHAPTER SIX

NOVEMBER

– NEWS UPDATE –

Bring on the Hatters

GAMES were coming thick and fast. Luton Town were next in line and Boro would be without Graeme Souness for the game at Ayresome Park.

Souness was starting a three match ban following his sending-off at Carlisle and was replaced by 17 year old Tony McAndrew, who was making his debut.

Explaining why McAndrew (right) was in ahead of Eric McMordie or Harry Charlton, Jack Charlton said: "I have been watching Tony a lot this season. He's got a lot to learn, but he's an honest lad and he's going to be a good player.

"He will play in the role I ask Souness to play, which I don't think the others could."

McAndrew was to leave for Largs on the Ayrshire coast the day after the game, linking up with the Scottish Youth Team.

John Hickton returned from a knee injury, Peter Brine making way.

Elsewhere Willie Carson became champion jockey for the second successive year.

Tony McAndrew: first team call up.

* * * * *

SATURDAY NOVEMBER 3
Middlesbrough 2   Luton Town 1

MIDDLESBROUGH	LUTON TOWN
Platt	Barber
Craggs	Shanks
Spraggon	Thomson
McAndrew	Anderson
Boam (Mills 30)	Faulkner
Maddren	Garner
Murdoch	Jimmy Ryan
Smith	Finney
Hickton	Butlin
Foggon	West
Armstrong	Aston
	Sub: John Ryan

Scorers: Butlin 32, Foggon 51, Armstrong 55.

Attendance: 22,590.

Match Report

LUTON were the more purposeful side from the start. A Jimmy Ryan free-kick found Peter Anderson unmarked, but the wing-half headed just wide. Tom Finney, a youngster with a famous name, brought a good save from Jim Platt.

Boro lost their captain Stuart Boam after half an hour. Boam had been up supporting a Boro attack when he landed awkwardly and was unable to continue. David Mills came off the bench, and John Hickton dropped back into defence.

However, Luton threw everything into attack and went a goal up two minutes later. Alan West cut in from the left wing, Boro backed off, and when West crossed into the goalmouth, Barry Butlin headed in from point blank range.

Charlton laid into his team during the half-time interval and Boro were a different side in the second 45 minutes.

It took just six minutes to equalise and a further four to take a match winning lead.

A left-wing cross from David Armstrong found Alan Foggon well placed to hammer in from close range on 51 minutes. John Craggs then sent David Mills clear and his cross to the far post brought a powerful header from Armstrong which gave Keith Barber no chance.

The game had turned on its head and Luton flew back at Boro. Finney hit a post and then shot just wide, while John Aston just failed to control the ball in front of goal.

Charlton, while happy with the result, was not enamoured with the performance, saying: "I was concerned about some of the basic things we did wrong. My coach, Ian MacFarlane, Stuart Boam and myself had a long talk and exchanged our views on what went wrong."

As for the Luton manager, Harry Haslam, he went a shade further, saying: "What happened out there left the Great Train Robbery standing! We played the football and they got the points. It was smash and grab."

– MAN OF THE MATCH –

HARRY Haslam was none too keen to offer any Boro player, but eventually conceded: "I only saw my players and the referee, but I suppose I would have to give it to MADDREN."

Stuart Boam, (No 5), leads from the front against the Hatters at Ayresome Park.

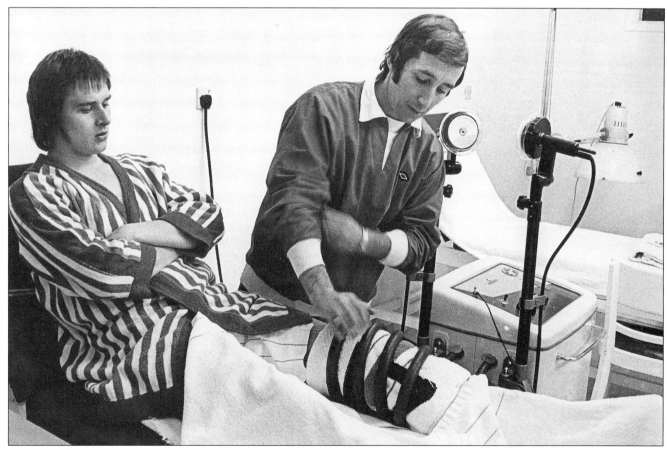

A look behind the scenes in the Ayresome Park treatment room as Peter Brine receives attention from trainer Jimmy Headrige.

– NEWS UPDATE –

Wonderful for Willie

STUART Boam declared himself fit on the morning of the League Cup replay against Stoke City.

The skipper's bruised hip suffered against Luton on Saturday had cleared up after treatment and he took his place in a side which showed two changes from that which won at the weekend.

Bill Gates started what was to be the first of only two matches in the season, replacing Tony McAndrew, while David Mills returned ahead of Malcolm Smith, who reverted to a substitute role.

Stoke had been beaten 2-1 at Newcastle on Saturday and John Ritchie had to pass a late fitness test on an sore calf to play against Boro, after picking up the injury at St James' Park.

There was good news for Willie Maddren (right), on the day of the cuptie, as he was named in a squad of 16 for a European Under-23 game against Denmark to be played at Portsmouth the following Tuesday.

In addition, Willie was voted Footballer Of The Month for September by the Daily Mirror, winning a trophy and a cheque for £100.

"It's great news," beamed Maddren. "It all seems to be happening for me at the moment. I would think my biggest rival for a place in the international side is West Ham's Kevin Lock, but we'll see."

Willie Maddren: England bound.

* * * * *

TUESDAY NOVEMBER 6

| Middlesbrough 1 | Stoke City 2 |
| | (after extra time) |

MIDDLESBROUGH	**STOKE CITY**
Platt	Farmer
Craggs	Marsh
Spraggon	Pejic
Gates	Mahoney
Boam	Smith
Maddren	Dodd
Murdoch	Skeels
Mills	Greenhoff
Hickton	Ritchie
Foggon	Hurst
Armstrong	Haselgrave
Sub: Smith	Sub: Goodwin

Scorers: Greenhoff 39, Foggon 80, Pejic 91.

Attendance: 26,068.

Match Report

BORO battled for 120 minutes against their First Division opponents, giving everything they had. Despite running themselves into the ground they could not find a way through a well organised team which created plenty of chances of its own.

Geoff Hurst missed a bagful and it was left to skipper Jimmy Greenhoff to put the visitors into the lead. The inside forward swivelled inside the penalty area to fire in a low shot off the post after 39 minutes.

Boro flew at Stoke with an all out attack mentality, but despite their pressure they didn't equalise until ten minutes from the end of normal time. Willie Maddren had a shot blocked, but Alan Foggon took his time to control the ball and slotted it past Farmer.

Boro's biggest crowd of the season watched both sides attack for all they were worth in extra-time, the winner coming in the first minute of the second period as left-back Mike Pejic blazed his way through to blast past Platt. This was enough to take Stoke, the winners from the season before last, through to round four.

"I couldn't have asked any more of the lads," said Charlton. "They fought and chased all through. At least we left the competition on a decent note."

They also left the field to a standing ovation.

– MAN OF THE MATCH –

TONY Waddington, the Stoke City manager, singled out DAVID ARMSTRONG, but failed to give a reason.

Future Boro midfielder John "Josh" Mahoney played a leading role in Stoke City's pulsating League Cup replay win at Ayresome Park.

– NEWS UPDATE –

Armstrong for England

TONY Waddington may have fought shy of praising Armstrong, but Boro's first team coach Ian MacFarlane extolled his virtues from the rooftops and also issued some prophetic words.

He said: "David Armstrong reminds me very forcibly of the young Jimmy Greaves, with whom I played in the Chelsea side.

"Their attitude to the game is exactly the same, but Jimmy's finishing is better! However David's workrate is a darned sight better! Armstrong must eventually play for England."

David Armstrong. Next stop England?

* * * * *

Five-a-side

THE League Cup replay meant Boro sent a weakened side to London for the prestigious Daily Express five-a-side tournament at Wembley Arena.

Boro, Sunderland, Celtic and Rangers were the only sides from outside of the First Division to be invited.

Boro lost 1-0 to Manchester United, a goal being set up by George Best and scored by Brian Greenhoff. Derby beat Celtic 3-1 in the final.

* * * * *

To the manor born

THE cup replay had also put paid to Boro's plans to travel to Oxford. They had originally intended to stay at Bisham Abbey after the five-a-side tournament, travelling to Oxford on the day of the match. Plan B was put into operation and Boro travelled on the Friday night.

The U's were struggling and had been beaten 2-1 at Bolton the previous Saturday. They were also without enigmatic striker Hugh Curran for the game against Boro.

Boro were unchanged from the side which lost to Stoke.

* * * * *

– MAN OF THE MATCH –

OXFORD boss Gerry Summers singled out STUART BOAM, simply saying: "The big lad did a lot of good work."

SATURDAY NOVEMBER 10
Oxford United 0   Middlesbrough 2

OXFORD UNITED	MIDDLESBROUGH
Burton	Platt
Lucas	Craggs
Shuker	Spraggon
Roberts	Gates
Clarke	Boam
Evanson	Maddren
Clarke	Murdoch
Jeffrey (Skeen 74)	Mills
Cassidy	Hickton
Gough	Foggon
Atkinson	Armstrong
	Sub: Brine

Scorers: Foggon 37, Murdoch 88.

Attendance: 8,733.

Match Report

BRILLIANT sunshine and a clear blue sky greeted the teams as they took the field at the Manor Ground.

It was Boro who attacked first. David Mills had a close range shot blocked, while a John Craggs piledriver deflected off centre-half Colin Clarke and hit the side netting with goalkeeper Roy Burton stranded.

Jim Platt needed to be agile to palm away a good effort from Bill Jeffrey, while Burton was lively at the other end in keeping out a low Bobby Murdoch effort.

It was an open enough game early on, but it was Boro who took the lead on 37 minutes.

A great through ball from Murdoch found Foggon, who whipped in a low first time strike beyond Burton.

Oxford wasted a chance to equalise minutes before half time as left half John Evanson shot over with the goal at his mercy.

Oxford battered away at Boro in the second half and inside left Keith Gough shot straight at Platt from the edge of the penalty area. Left winger Graham Atkinson lobbed straight at the Boro 'keeper, while Gough failed to make the best of a rare error by Willie Maddren.

Right-half Dai Roberts had a close range header cleared off the line by John Craggs, but it was Boro who broke to seal the game in the final minute. John Hickton swept from one end of the field to the other, drawing 'keeper Burton and squaring to Murdoch, who sidefooted into an empty net with 50 seconds remaining.

Craggs and Mills were booked for Boro, the first time two players had been booked in the same game that season.

Oxford United v Middlesbrough
Saturday 10th November

*Oxford's Dave Roberts, right, is at full stretch to thwart John Hickton's goal-bound strike at the Manor Ground.
Bill Gates, playing in his only league start of the season, is on hand to lend Big John some support.*

– NEWS UPDATE –

Traitors

OXFORD chairman, Bob Kersey, launched a stinging attack on Boro, condemning them as "traitors to the game", adding: "If they keep playing like that they'll be hated on every ground in the country."

The Boro chairman, Charles Amer (right), retorted: "For too long we have been one of the most courteous clubs in the country and one of the nicest without winning anything.

"Well we can still be gentlemen, but we can win. I deplore the inflammatory remarks made by the Oxford chairman which are hardly conducive to keeping peace on the terraces.

"It is Jack Charlton's brand of football which is starting to come out now and who knows, it may be more exciting than anything we have had before.

Amer anger.

"Is anyone going to suggest we haven't seen possession football at Ayresome Park this season? We don't go away to hang on to a point. We have won more games than anyone away from home. Is that negative? We simply have the best defence in the division."

Boro found an ally from elsewhere in the league. The Carlisle manager Alan Ashman sprang to their defence, saying: "If any manager can take his team to the top of the division, then they can't be playing bad football. I certainly wouldn't complain if Carlisle were in the same position."

They were currently eight points away in seventh place.

He added: "There's nothing new about the way Boro play. Someone does it every year, but Boro do it well."

* · * · * · * · *

Powerless

IT was a busy week leading up to Boro's next game.

Princess Anne and Captain Mark Phillips were married at Westminster Abbey. The miners' strike was beginning to hurt nationwide, while there was still terrible conflict in Northern Ireland, with bombings on mainland Britain still a massive threat.

Boro had been lucky earlier in the season. Two days after playing away to Crystal Palace, they, like the nation, were shocked when a massive bomb ripped through Kings Cross station, the main station for journeys to the North of England.That bomb could have gone off at any time.

The miners' strike was having an effect on fuel. There was a general shortage and the country was rationed with the amount it could use, especially electricity. Football was no exception. The government of the day would not grant permission to use generators, saying they used too much petrol and therefore the use of floodlights was banned.

Boro's game at home to Cardiff City was to kick-off an hour earlier than normal at 2pm.

* * * * *

Award for Shep

Boro's assistant manager Harold Shepherdson became only the fifth man in history to receive a silver salver from the FA in appreciation of services given over a long period of time.

The only other recipients were Billy Wright, Bobby Moore, Bobby Charlton and Sir Alf Ramsey.

Shepherdson was awarded the salver prior to England's friendly international with Italy at Wembey on the Wednesday night.

The inscription on the salver said it all: "To Harold Shepherdson from the FA in appreciation of loyal service and to mark his 150th appearance as trainer of England from 1957-1972."

The Italy game was in fact his 161st with England. Despite the recognition, there was no overnight stop for Shep. He caught the train immediately after the game, arriving home at three in the morning.

* * * * *

Ticket sale

BORO announced that they were to sell cut priced season tickets to cover the last 12 games of the season. The tickets would be priced £8.50, £7.50 and £6.50, with only a limited number available.

* * * * *

Bluebird bashing

CARDIFF had sacked their manager Jimmy Scoular on November 7 and their first game under new boss Frank O'Farrell brought the lowest crowd since the war to Ninian Park, with just under 6,000 watching a goalless draw with Luton in driving rain.

Former Boro players George Smith and Johnny Vincent were with Cardiff now. Smith was injured and missed the game, while Vincent was substitute.

Boro made two changes to the side for the first time this season. They welcomed back Graeme Souness from suspension. He replaced Bill Gates, while Eric McMordie played his first game since the middle of September as Bobby Murdoch had a sore knee. It was the last time the Irishman would start a game in a Boro shirt.

Alan Foggon was keen to prove a point against a club which had sold him to Boro for £10,000 the previous season.

* * * * *

SATURDAY NOVEMBER 17

Middlesbrough 3   Cardiff City 0

MIDDLESBROUGH	CARDIFF CITY
Platt	Irwin
Craggs	Dwyer
Spraggon	Bell
Souness	Impey (Vincent 72)
Boam	Murray
Maddren	Phillips
McMordie	Villars
Mills	McInch
Hickton	Showers
Foggon (Smith 25)	Woodruff
Armstrong	Powell

Scorers: Mills 36, Craggs 86, Smith 89.

Attendance: 18,034.

Match Report

BORO blamed the early start for the comparatively poor gate. On the field there was a brisk start from Boro, left-back Frank Spraggon popping up with the game's first shot in the opening minutes.

Boro had a penalty appeal turned down and Eric McMordie blasted over the bar as the home side dominated the early exchanges. Alan Foggon damaged a calf muscle after 21 minutes and was replaced by Malcolm Smith, but Boro kept up the pressure.

The breakthrough came after 36 minutes. A David Mills header was half saved by Irwin, but was scrambled over the line by the Boro forward.

McInch suddenly burst clear to cause Boro an unexpected problem, but he wasted his opportunity and shot wide. It had developed into a patchy game long before Boro almost doubled their advantage when a Hickton shot was cleared off the line by Dwyer.

Boro were in complete command when they rattled in two goals in three of the last four minutes. John Craggs dispatched a left footed swerver beyond the reach of Irwin on 86 minutes, while Malcolm Smith gave the scoreline a more realistic look when scoring from close range three minutes later.

David Mills bravely ignores the flying Cardiff City boots to head towards goal.

Second Division League Table - 23-11-73

	P	W	D	L	F	A	Pts
MIDDLESBROUGH	**15**	**9**	**5**	**1**	**16**	**8**	**23**
Aston Villa	15	7	6	2	23	12	20
Orient	15	5	8	2	23	15	18
Notts County	14	7	4	3	21	17	18
Bristol City	15	7	3	5	18	15	17
Nottingham Forest	15	5	6	4	22	13	16

– NEWS UPDATE –

Canada Bound

JACK Charlton had spent most of the week leading up to the next game, at Notts County, out of the country.

Charlton, together with brother Bobby, Jimmy Greaves and Gordon Banks, had flown to Canada to help launch an indoor soccer league.

He returned to find Alan Foggon out of the starting line up. His place was taken by Peter Brine, while Bobby Murdoch returned from injury in place of Malcolm Smith.

County named an unchanged side for the 14th successive game and had been beaten only once at home all season, by Sunderland in September.

* * * * *

SATURDAY NOVEMBER 24

Notts County 2   Middlesbrough 2

NOTTS COUNTY	**MIDDLESBROUGH**
McManus	Platt
Brindley	Craggs
Worthington	Spraggon
Masson	Souness
Needham	Boam
Stubbs	Maddren
Nixon	Murdoch
Randall	Brine
Bradd	Mills
Probert	Hickton
Mann	Armstrong
Sub: Vinter	Sub: Smith

Scorers: Bradd 31, Masson 41, Hickton 46, Mills 59.

Attendance: 16,314.

Match Report

A strong swirling wind made life difficult for players, but it was County who were first to settle.

Randall had already struck the top of the bar before the home side opened the scoring after 31 minutes.

Nixon moved well down the right, carried on unchecked by any Boro player and sent over a fine cross which was headed in by Bradd from close range.

County, in fifth place in the table, were looking good and went two up shortly before half-time.

Another right-wing cross from Nixon caused problems, Platt and Masson rose together, with Masson - a former Boro player (61 appearances) - getting there first.

Shortly before half-time Armstrong had a shot cleared of the line to give Boro hope.

That hope was turned into reality within the opening 14 minutes of the second half. A minute into the restart Souness took a corner on the right, Boam headed it down and Hickton turned it in from close range.

Boro drew level after 59 minutes. Constant pressure resulted in a melee inside the County penalty area and Mills turned a loose ball into the net.

– MAN OF THE MATCH –

County Manager Jimmy Sirrell nominated
DAVID MILLS for his hard work and industry

The Notts County side captained by former Middlesbrough midfielder Don Masson, front row third right, which held high flying Boro to a 2-2 draw at Meadow Lane.

REFLECTIONS

Stuart Boam & Willie Maddren

THE captain led by example. Stuart Boam was a no-nonsense up and at 'em player who found few in the opposition who argued with him.

"I think I was made captain because I had the biggest mouth," he jokes.

"Maybe there was something of Jack which he saw in me, I don't know, but I didn't expect to be made captain all the same."

When Nobby Stiles left to join Preston without kicking a ball that season, Boro were in need of a new skipper.

The choice appeared to lie between Boam and Willie Maddren.

"Jack had spent all summer telling me how bad I was, how I couldn't kick a ball and how I would never make a decent centre-half.

"We had some right up and downers, but he always got his point across, which was clearly that he didn't rate me at all.

"I didn't know whether he had come as a player/manager and would therefore be taking my position and it wasn't a smooth summer.

"Then, on the morning of the opening game of the season, at Portsmouh, Jack pulled me to one side and told me I was captain!"

Maddren took the news badly, not that he didn't rate Boam, it was sheer disappointment at not achieving a dream.

"I thought Willie was a certainty," confesses Boam. "He was a local lad, he had all the talent in the world and he would have made a good leader, I'm sure.

"I well remember walking along Southsea sea front two hours before kick-off, consoling Willie. He was crying his eyes out. I've never told anyone that before. But come kick-off time there wasn't a problem. The true professional that he was he just got on with his job."

Boam and Maddren formed a formidable partnership. Yet they didn't start the season together. Brian Taylor was first choice centre-half alongside the skipper, while Maddren played in midfield.

An injury to Taylor in the fourth match of the season inadvertently brought together a rock which was seldom passed.

While there were few changes to the side throughout the season, only three players were ever present, Boam, Maddren and David Armstrong.

In the 38 games Boam and Maddren played together in the centre of Boro's defence, only 26 goals were scored against them and seven of those were in the last four games!

To make the statistic even more impressive comes another confession from Boam.

"We only used to train together once a week normally. Because of the state of Willie's knees he would never train as much as we did. Therefore we only used to work together on defensive routines on the Thursday before every game when the pair of us, and one or two others, would stay back after regular training."

The remarkable understanding they had together must have been telepathic. Indeed they were often known as the Telepathic Twins.

"We complemented each other. Willie was phenomenal. He was the better footballer by a mile. I'm convinced it was only his knees which prevented him from playing a leading role with the England set up. He was one of the best footballers in the country and it was a privilege to be playing alongside him.

"I could maybe do certain things better than he could. I could handle the big lads. But it was the little ones which got in under you feet that I had problems with!"

Boam says that one player elsewhere on the pitch had more than a significant contribution to make to the success of the team, in addition to Jack.

"There's no doubt about it, Bobby Murdoch was a world class player. His pace had left him a bit when he joined us, but he was still a world class player who had a major influence on us. He was an inspiration and motivator to us all.

"So was Jack, he was brilliant motivator. You would tend to want to do it for Jack. He was like part of the lads, but not part of the lads if you see what I mean. Jack was just far enough away not to be one of us altogether.

"He encouraged us off the park as well. He sometimes went a bit too far over the line, but he quickly stepped back again.

"He always used make training fun, sometimes unintentionally. He could never remember his own team's names half the time, never mind the opposition. We often used to scream with laughter. But he knew what he wanted.

"He always said that the central defenders of a team were the labourers and the rest were the technicians. He never changed from the day I met him to the day he finished with the Irish team.

"But I still remember that team talk in the Marton Country Club. He praised everybody, he straightened out Graeme Souness, who couldn't get a game because he was fannying about, he rightly praised the rest, saved me 'til last and then slaughtered me.

"It was a man management skill. He took me down to the depths, just to shoot me to the heights. I realise that now, but I'll tell you now I went home after that meeting and threw up. I was physically sick.

"But from that day on we had a great respect for each other. He has never changed and never will. He's a great guy, but he'll never stop dressing like a tramp and never stop getting soup down his tie, which was always a trademark!

"He'll never change and I like him for that and I'll tell you what, I wouldn't give the England manager's job to anybody else, even now.

"Remember when he took over it wasn't a case of would we win the league, it was a case of would we survive.

"We were a team who hadn't played together that much. We started off as nobodies, but we had potential and through Jack we realised that potential."

Boam concludes with a rare praiseful mention of the press who followed Boro at the time.

Cliff Mitchell of the Evening Gazette and Ray Robertson of the Northern Echo were the chief reporters. They had the respect of the players, as Boam explains: "We had the utmost respect for them. They were gentlemen in every sense of the word.

"They travelled all over on the bus with us and knew what to write and what not to write. A punch on the training ground was news, a punch on the bus on the way home from a match wasn't. Not that it ever happened, but that was just an example of the way they operated.

"They did their job, did it well and through that gained the respect of the players. There are too many these days who don't command that respect."

The Telepathic Twins in a light-hearted training session with local youngsters.

CHAPTER SEVEN

DECEMBER

Frost and snow bring north end blow

THREE local companies, Whessoe, JW Morgan and JD White, helped Boro in their search for a generator ahead of their next match, at home to Preston, with Boro hopeful of gaining permission for its use from the government.

It was to be the first time in English club history that brothers had managed in direct opposition to one another, Bobby being the manager of Preston North End.

But the weather grew colder the longer the week went on and on the Friday before the game the temperature in Middlesbrough had dropped to minus-eight degrees. It was positively tropical compared with Carlisle, where it had dropped to -23!

BBC TV's Match Of The Day was to show the game, the first time Boro were to be featured that season.

However, overnight, Teesside shivered in the coldest December for 11 years. Overnight the temperature had dropped to -14, equivalent to 25 degrees farenheit of frost.

By 9am the temperature had risen only by two degrees, and 55 minutes later the game was formally called off.

Although Boro were not playing, their position at the top of the table was consolidated as second placed Orient lost 2-1 at home to Cardiff City.

On their way back home, two Boro players were involved in a car accident. Both Jim Platt and Bobby Murdoch lived in Redcar. Platt was giving Murdoch a lift when, driving at "a snail's pace", he skidded on very icy roads and ran into the back of another car. Fortunately there was nothing damaged except the car radiator.

*   *   *   *   *

Spraggon suffering as Owls force draw

FRANK Spraggon had been suffering from a stomach complaint during the build up to Boro's next match, at Sheffield Wednesday. On the eve of the game he was taken into North Ormesby Hospital after passing blood in his urine.

Jimmy Cochrane was called up to make his debut. Cochrane, a 20 year old from Drumchapel, went on to appear just four times for Boro before being transferred to Darlington.

The Wednesday chairman, Sir Andrew Stephen, had resigned on the Thursday before the match following strong criticism from fans, disgruntled at their side's placing at the foot of the table. Vice-chairman Keith Gardiner also resigned, leaving 49 year old accountant Matt Sheppard in charge.

*   *   *   *   *

Young Boro defender Jimmy Cochrane made his debut at Hillsborough in place of the hospitalised Frank Spraggon.

Match Report

BORO opened well with David Armstrong in the thick of the action. Early in the game he split the defence with a ball to John Hickton, but his shot found Peter Springett well placed.

A solo effort from Armstrong went inches wide as Boro looked promising, but it was Wednesday who took the lead after 20 minutes. Inside-left Michael Prendergast latched on to a right-wing cross to send a left footed shot past Jim Platt, who appeared to have the ball covered until it bounced awkwardly in front of him.

Boro equalised seven minutes from the break. Former Wednesday player Hickton set off on an electrifying run down the left. He sent over a low cross and with three waiting in the middle, it was Alan Foggon who assumed responsibility and slid the ball past Springett.

Jimmy Cochrane was enjoying an excellent debut, checking the runs of ex-Rangers and Scotland international Willie Henderson. However, the one time he was beaten it led to a goal, Henderson delivering a low cross which was turned in after 57 minutes by centre-forward Brian Joicey.

Boro fought back and had a series of attacks repelled until the 70th minute. John Craggs moved upfield in menacing fashion and crossed to David Mills, who blasted a first time shot into the net.

That set up a grandstand finish by Boro, but they couldn't add to their tally.

Jack Charlton wasn't too happy with the result, even though his side had avoided defeat, saying: "The goals we scored were the end product of constructive football, whereas the Wednesday goals had an element of luck about them."

Boro's lead was cut to three points at the top of the Second Division as Orient, having rattled in three in five minutes, went on to win 4-2 at Notts County.

SATURDAY DECEMBER 8
Sheffield Wednesday 2   Middlesbrough 2

SHEFFIELD WEDNESDAY	MIDDLESBROUGH
Springett	Platt
Rodrigues	Craggs
Shaw	Cochrane
Thompson	Souness
Mullen	Boam
Craig	Maddren
Henderson	Murdoch
Knighton	Mills
Joicey	Hickton
Prendergast	Foggon
Potts	Armstrong
Sub: Sunley	Sub: Brine

Scorers: Prendergast 20, Foggon 38, Joicey 57, Mills 70.

Attendance: 11,968.

– MAN OF THE MATCH –

STUART BOAM won the vote of Wednesday manager Derek Dooley. His explanation: "He was very commanding in the centre of the defence."

Suits you sir! Double breasted jackets and flared trousers are the fashion of the day as the Boro Boys step out in style.

– NEWS UPDATE –

History in the making

AT last Jackie and Bobby were to meet as managers. Boro had been given the go-ahead to use a generator to power the floodlights at Ayresome Park and would meet Preston North End in a re-arranged game.

Both brothers played down the meeting, the first time in English club history that brothers had to come face to face as opposition managers. Both agreed it was: "Just another game."

Preston included Ray Treacy, a striker who cost £30,000 from Swindon Town, and Nobby Stiles, who had left Boro before kicking a ball in anger this season.

Thankfully Frank Spraggon had been given the all clear and was able to return to action, otherwise Boro were unchanged from the side which had drawn at Hillsborough.

* * * * *

Brother Bobby's Preston were no match for Jack's Boro as the men from Deepdale were crushed 3-0 in a one-sided encounter.

TUESDAY DECEMBER 11
Middlesbrough 3   Preston North End 0

MIDDLESBROUGH	PRESTON NORTH END
Platt	Healey
Craggs	McMahon
Spraggon	Bird
Souness	Sadler
Boam	McNab (Hawkins 66)
Maddren	Stiles
Murdoch	Treacy
Mills	Lamb
Hickton	Bruce
Foggon	Burns
Armstrong	Young
Sub: Smith	

Scorers: Mills 15, Murdoch 22, Souness 87.

Attendance: 23,980.

Match Report

MR and Mrs Charlton watched impassively from the directors' box as Boro comfortably brushed aside an ordinary Preston side with the scoreline being an accurate reflection of Boro's superiority.

Bobby Murdoch was outstanding, while Graeme Souness linked well with David Mills and John Hickton, whose front running was a feature of the game.

It was Mills who put Boro into the lead after 15 minutes, a low rasping drive giving Healey no chance. Boro went two-up on 22 minutes, another low drive, this time from Murdoch, beating the 'keeper.

It came as something of a surprise that Boro had to wait until three minutes from time before the scoreline took on something like respectibility, Souness dispatching a rising drive into the back of the net.

The only downbeat note for Boro was a booking picked up by John Craggs, who now faced suspension.

Nobby Stiles was full of compliments for his ex-team mates after the game, saying: "The lads really turned it on. They played magnificently in the opening 25 minutes and tore us to shreds. No side will touch them in the promotion race."

> ## – MAN OF THE MATCH –
> *BOBBY Charlton offered the following assessment of DAVID MILLS, who was given the nomination: "He was the most dangerous forward on view."*

– NEWS UPDATE –

Strike a light

THE country was grinding to a halt. A series of stoppages were having a devastating effect, with the miners' strike the most crippling of all, with many homes having to do without power at certain times of the day.

The railways were on strike, which meant that Exeter, who were playing away to Workington on the Saturday, had to set off at 9am on the Friday to make sure they arrived in time, as all motor vehicles were restricted to 50mph.

The Middlesbrough Evening Gazette journalists were on strike, while BBC and ITV were told to shut down by 10.30 at night.

The government, whose Chancellor, Mr Barber, had described the conditions as " the worst position this country has been in since the end of the war", reimposed a ban on generators.

This caused a storm with certain clubs, especially Millwall and Tottenham. Millwall had paid £1,000 for the hire of a generator, while Tottenham had bought theirs for £10,000.

The announcement was only made at 12.17pm on the Friday before the weekend's fixtures, which all had to kick-off at 2pm.

Boro chairman, Charles Amer, said: "It's surely not too much to ask that a dozen or so football matches, where generators were to be used, should be allowed to carry on to cater for the millions of fans who find relaxation in sport.

"Today for instance, if all the clubs which wanted to, had been permitted to use emergency power equipment, the total consumption would have been less than 200 gallons.

"The generator at Ayresome Park has a fuel tank with a capacity of 60 gallons - more than enough for three matches, as we estimate useage of 16 gallons a match."

*   *   *   *   *

Forest fire next to be extinguished

BORO were unchanged for the game against Nottingham Forest, who included the division's leading scorer Duncan McKenzie, who had found the net 13 times so far.

Northern Ireland international Martin O'Neill played at inside left in a side showing one change from the one which drew 1-1 at Cardiff the previous week.

*   *   *   *   *

SATURDAY DECMEBER 15
Middlesbrough 1   Nottingham Forest 0

MIDDLESBROUGH	NOTTINGHAM FOREST
Platt	Barron
Craggs	O'Kane
Spraggon	Winfield
Souness	Chapman
Boam	Cottam
Maddren	Richardson
Murdoch	McKenzie
Mills	Lyall
Hickton	Martin
Foggon	O'Neill
Armstrong	Bowyer
Sub: Smith	Sub: Hindley

Scorer: Boam 30.

Attendance: 16,764.

Match Report

BORO widened the gap at the top of the table with this vital win as nearest rivals Orient lost 1-0 at home to Carlisle. Luton moved into second place with a 1-0 home win over Aston Villa.

The Ayresome Park pitch had a light covering of snow, with some flakes swirling around in an icy cold wind. An hour before kick-off the referee had asked for the lines to be coloured blue, but there wasn't enough time, so the snow was cleared from each touchline.

The players moved gingerly in the opening manoeuvres, with Boro's central defensive duo, Stuart Boam and Willie Maddren, both making errors.

John Craggs, however, carried on as normal, making telling runs which had the Forest defence struggling. It was a defender who proved to be the match winner as Nottinghamshire-born Stuart Boam found the back of the net just short of the half hour.

Liam O'Kane received a booking for a foul on David Mills. David Armstrong floated in a dangerous free-kick to which Boam rose high to head in just below the crossbar.

Boro were mounting more pressure as the first half drew to a close, with another Forest player, Bob Chapman, booked for a dangerous play.

A minute into the restart and Forest were down to ten men when O'Kane, previously booked, was sent-off for a dangerous foul on Armstrong.

Boro, with the wind at their backs and numerical supremacy, took the game to Forest with Durham-born Jim Barron producing an outstanding save to deny Graeme Souness.

Boro left themselves wide open just short of the hour mark when Duncan McKenzie rattled the crossbar, but that was the closest the visitors came to scoring.

Assessing the match, Charlton said: "The conditions ruined the game. It was OK in the first half when the snow was on the ground, but when the sleet came it was impossible.

"Given the conditions, the best thing about the day was the result. It was good to get the game out of the way."

At the half-way point of the season Boro were six points clear of second placed Luton, who had a game in hand, seven ahead of third placed Orient, who had played the same number of games, and nine ahead of fourth placed Notts County, who had played one game fewer.

Martin O'Neill exacted his revenge over twenty years later when his Leicester City side beat Middlesbrough in the Coca Cola Cup Final.

– MAN OF THE MATCH –

THE Forest trainer, John McSeveney, nominated DAVID ARMSTRONG, saying: "He always did the job right in a straightforward manner and caused us most trouble."

- NEWS UPDATE -

Up for the Cup

BORO were drawn away to Grantham or Rochdale in the third round of the FA Cup. The odds were on Rochdale as the two sides had drawn at Grantham on the Saturday. The replay was to take place 48 hours later at Spotland.

Normally Charlton didn't bother watching opponents before a game, but this time was an exception, but not for any football reasons.

Charlton was due to speak at a testimonial dinner for Billy Bremner in Blackpool on the evening of the replay, which was to be played in the afternoon. So he decided he would take in the game along the way!

Although they were favourites, Rochdale had a dreadful home record. They had won none, drawn five and lost four. Incredibly Southern League Grantham won 5-3 after extra-time after being two down in the opening six minutes of the match.

Discussions were then held about switching the tie against Middlesbrough to Ayresome Park as Grantham's London Road ground held only 6,500.

The final decision was that the game would be played at Grantham, and 2,500 standing tickets were made available to Boro fans, but no seats.

Boro rejected the chance to switch the game to a Sunday, with director George Kitching saying: "If the game were to be switched to a Sunday, our fans would have to leave early in the morning and miss their traditional Sunday lunch."

Prices were increased by 20p to 50p, with seats for the home fans doubled in price to 70p.

But there were three league games to fit in beforehand. One was against Sunderland. Confirmation was received from the government that the derby game, scheduled for Boxing Day, could go ahead under floodlights as special arrangements had been made for power rationing over the Chrsitmas period, provided a licence was obtained.

The country, meanwhile, had been put on a three-day week with electricity available on only four full days. There were to be power cuts on Thursdays, Fridays and Saturdays.

Boro's home game with Crystal Palace, scheduled for December 29, would kick-off at 2pm as there was no permission granted for the use of lights on that day.

*   *   *   *   *

All square at Ashton Gate

JOHN Craggs started a two match suspension and missed the game at Bristol City, his place being taken by Peter Creamer, a 20 year old defender from Hartlepool, who was starting a game for the first time that season.

Creamer had previously made six appearances for Boro, but was to make only three this time around.

Bristol City, who had won at Cardiff the previous week, had one of the youngest captains in the league in 22 year old Geoff Merrick. He had recently been the subject of a £100,000 bid from Nottingham Forest.

*   *   *   *   *

Jack Charlton continued to give youth its head when he gave Peter Creamer his debut at Ashton Gate in place of the suspended John Craggs.

SATURDAY DECEMBER 22

Bristol City 1   Middlesbrough 1

BRISTOL CITY	**MIDDLESBROUGH**
Bond	Platt
Sweeney	Creamer
Merrick	Spraggon
Emanuel	Souness
Rodgers (Burrell 51)	Boam
Collier	Maddren
Tainton	Murdoch
Ritchie	Mills
Gillies	Hickton
Gow	Foggon
Fear	Armstrong
	Sub: Brine

Scorers: Mills 5, Gillies 59.

Attendance: 13,116.

- MAN OF THE MATCH -

CITY boss Alan Dicks couldn't split STUART BOAM and WILLIE MADDREN, saying: "Every time we broke into the penalty area, which was quite often, these two stood firm and worked well together."

Match Report

BORO'S longest trip of the season brought about an almost immediate reward. Bobby Murdoch found David Mills with a defence splitting pass and Mills collected the ball just inside the penalty area, steadied himself, and then unleashed a fierce drive beyond Len Bond after only five minutes.

City hit back, John Emanuel shooting just over, while Tom Ritchie shot inches wide through a crowded penalty area.

Boro almost scored again early in the second half. John Hickton and Alan Foggon had been close in the closing stages of the opening 45 minutes, and Foggon was close again, being inches away from a teasing cross.

A minute later City equalised. Mills, attempting a back-pass from almost on the half-way line, hit it straight to Don Gillies, who couldn't believe his luck. Gathering the ball, he hammered it past Jim Platt after 59 minutes.

City, with their tails up, were unlucky not to be awarded a penalty minutes later as Armstrong clearly handled inside the box, but the home side were merely awarded a free-kick on the edge of the area.

Boro cleared that effort, but City went close on a number of occasions. Even so Boro almost snatched it when an Armstrong shot was cleared off the line by right-back Gerry Sweeney.

Mills was questioned about the backpass after the game, explaining his side of the story: "I thought the way was clear back to our 'keeper. The lads asked me if I had remembered that we had changed ends at half-time!

"But they told me not to feel too bad, as if I hadn't played then the game would have been a boring 0-0 affair!"

The City manager Alan Dicks said: "In the first half Boro looked the part of league leaders, but in the second we came right back at them and should have had a penalty."

Jimmy Greenhalgh (Junior Coach)

The hardworking backroom boys, left to right: Jimmy Headrige (Trainer), Harold Shepherdson (Assistant Manager), Ian MacFarlane (Chief Coach), Ron Ashwell, George Wardle and above Jimmy Greenhalgh (Junior Coaches).

- NEWS UPDATE -

Merry Christmas

SUNDERLAND at Ayresome Park on Boxing Day were Boro's next opponents and the build up to the game was far from smooth. Both Bobby Murdoch and Alan Foggon were unable to train on Christmas Eve, while Graeme Souness had both calves strapped.

Foggon had slightly strained knee ligaments, which tightened up on the long journey back from Bristol, while Murdoch was feeling "tender".

Former Sunderland coach Ian MacFarlane outlined the feeling in the camp when saying: "We have had a good work out and had some hard words after Bristol City.

"We are top of the table, but are under no illusions about the size of the task ahead. Our attitudes have to be the same in the second half of the season. Rest assured our players will be running themselves into the ground."

The day of the game was David Armstrong's 19th birthday. He was a Sunderland fan as a lad, but nailed his colours firmly to the mast ahead of this eagerly awaited contest.

He said: "It would be great if I got a combined birthday and Christmas present in the shape of two points. This is the match I want to win most of all."

David Armstrong: Birthday boy.

*   *   *   *   *

WEDNESDAY DECEMBER 26
Middlesbrough 2   Sunderland 1

MIDDLESBROUGH	**SUNDERLAND**
Platt	Swinburne
Creamer	Malone
Spraggon	Guthrie
Souness	Belfitt
Boam	Watson
Maddren	Young
Murdoch	Kerr
Mills	Hughes
Hickton (Smith 73)	Halom
Foggon	Porterfield
Armstrong	Tueart
	Sub: Ashurst

Scorers: Foggon 38, Tueart 41, Boam 88.

Attendance: 37,038.

Match Report

BORO equalled a club record 21 games without defeat with a late winner against their closest rivals - geographically speaking.

The largest crowd of the season by some considerable distance packed into Ayresome, but didn't see a classic.

The referee spoilt the game with constant whistle blowing and finicky decisions, although Boro just about deserved to win and their fans taunted their opposite numbers by offering a rendition of Slade's 1973 hit Merry Christmas Everybody.

Both Bobby Murdoch and Alan Foggon had been passed fit to play on the morning of the game as Boro named the same team which had done battle at Bristol.

Sunderland were without regular goalkeeper Jimmy Montgomery, who had injured a shoulder, with Trevor Swinburne standing in as deputy. It was his mistake which lead to the opening goal after 38 minutes. David Armstrong took a corner, Swinburne started to come for it, hesitated, and Alan Foggon took advantage by heading home.

It took Sunderland just three minutes to equalise. They were awarded a penalty from a dubious refereeing decision when Frank Spraggon was adjudged to have brought down Dennis Tueart. The same player picked himself up to equalise from the spot.

Sunderland were indebted to Bobby Kerr, whose workrate in midfield kept Boro from running amok, although Graeme Souness did spread the ball around well.

Boro felt they had won a penalty when David Mills was brought down, but the referee waved play on, soon after booking Mills for dissent.

Boro's winner came one minute and 40 seconds from the end of the game. Boro won a throw in on the right, Mills switched the ball inside and Stuart Boam, ghosting into space, brought it under control, picked his spot and hit a fierce drive into the net.

The Boro skipper ran from the East End of the ground, where he had scored the goal, to the Holgate End to receive the acclaim of an ecstatic crowd!

"The referee made some strange decisions," said Charlton. "Still, this is the one the lads wanted to win and I'm delighted they did."

The Sunderland manager saw it differently. Bob Stokoe lamented: "We deserved something from the match. Everything is in Boro's court now this season. They are a good solid team, but I thought they got the breaks today."

> ### - MAN OF THE MATCH -
>
> *BOB Stokoe eventually singled out STUART BOAM, saying: "It isn't easy to single anyone out, as Boro are a very good team.*
> *"But I thought Boam had a great game. He battled well all the way through and then came up with the winning goal."*

Middlesbrough v Sunderland Wednesday 26th December

Take that: Man of the Match, Boro skipper Stuart Boam, rifles home a late late winner against local rivals Sunderland which consolidated his side's position at the top of the table.

Second Division League Table - 24-12-73

	P	W	D	L	F	A	Pts
MIDDLESBROUGH	**21**	**13**	**7**	**1**	**29**	**12**	**33**
Luton Town	20	11	5	4	33	24	27
Orient	21	9	8	4	33	21	26
Notts County	20	9	6	5	34	30	24
Blackpool	21	9	5	7	28	22	23
West Bromwich Albion	21	8	7	6	23	22	23

– NEWS UPDATE –

Record Breakers

IT was top against bottom as Boro went for a club record 22 games without defeat. Crystal Palace were the next visitors to Ayresome Park, just three days after the win over Sunderland.

Boro had accumulated three times as many points as their London rivals and welcomed back John Craggs (right) after suspension.

Peter Creamer made way, with Charlton saying: "The lad played really well in both matches when John was suspended. At no time did he let us down. But it is true to say we missed the attacking flair of Craggs."

John Craggs returned after suspension.

Palace's towering centre-half Mel Blyth missed the game after twisting a knee in a 3-0 Boxing Day defeat at Orient. Ben Anderson took his place.

Boro's previous best unbeaten run was between November 20, 1926, and April 4, 1927, a run which started and ended with wins at Fulham. Boro's current run started with a win over today's opponents Crystal Palace.

On the same day that Boro played Palace, Leeds set an all-time First Division record of 23 games without defeat when drawing 1-1 at Birmingham, equalising in the closing minutes in front of 48,000 at St Andrews.

* * * * *

SATURDAY DECEMBER 29
Middlesbrough 2   Crystal Palace 0

MIDDLESBROUGH	CRYSTAL PALACE
Platt	Hammond
Craggs	Mulligan
Spraggon	Jump
Souness	Anderson
Boam	Barry
Maddren	Johnson
Murdoch	Jeffries
Mills	Lindsay
Hickton (Smith 78)	Hill
Foggon	Rogers
Armstrong	Taylor
	Sub: Wall

Scorers: Foggon 20, Armstrong 22.

Attendance: 26,115.

Match Report

AS soon as Boro opened the scoring there was never any doubt that they would set a new club record.

They took the game to Palace from the off, making light of the awkward windy conditions, Alan Foggon having a swerving shot saved by Paul Hammond.

Derek Jeffries made Jim Platt produce a fine save minutes later, the Boro 'keeper grabbing at the foot of a post. That proved to be against the run of play. John Craggs burst through on several occasions and it was a surprise that it took Boro 20 minutes to open the scoring, Graeme Souness playing the ball through to Foggon, whose accurate finish gave Hammond no chance.

Two minutes later Boro were two-up and cruising. A corner from Frank Spraggon was punched out by Hammond, but only as far as David Armstrong, who neatly headed past the despairing 'keeper.

Palace did well to avoid being turned over. Boro were much the better side with Bobby Murdoch, John Hickton, David Mills and John Craggs all shooting just wide.

The fingertips of Hammond denied Mills later in the game, while Foggon missed a sitter.

Armstrong was next to be frustrated, being just wide with a fine effort, while Souness had a powerful drive blocked.

"We kept things going and there was no hint of complacency," said Charlton "Some of the football we played was great stuff, especially as the game was played in difficult conditions."

– MAN OF THE MATCH –

EAGLES manager Malcolm Allison was not in talkative mood afterwards. When asked to nominate a Boro player he simply said: "Your No.11, DAVID ARMSTRONG." Allison, under pressure after his side had taken just 12 points from 24 matches, said he was ready to resign. Allison, who was being paid £13,000 a year, had spent what was a large amount of money in those days, £300,000, since the club had been relegated the previous season. Palace were now £500,000 in the red.

Alan Foggon celebrates scoring the opening goal against Crystal Palace at Ayresome Park.

REFLECTIONS
Graeme Souness

The fact that Graeme Souness didn't start the season, was the only player to be sent-off, missed games through suspension and still was voted Player Of The Year says it all.

Souness was, by his own admission, a player with an attitude. It was one which was changed, honed, by Jack Charlton.

"I had signed for Stan Anderson and quickly got him the sack!" says the Scot. "I proved to be his last signing before he left. Shep took over until the summer when Jack arrived.

"We were all left under no illusions that there was just one way of doing things, Jack's way. There was no room for argument. He was a large figure with a mouth to match and I mean that in the kindest sense.

"Players were 'invited' to train during the summer, two days a week, or more, but I went away on holiday, reported back overweight and suffered.

"Eric McMordie and myself thought we knew better, thought we could take Jack on and do what we wanted, Jack the Lad style if you like.

"I don't think Jack liked Eric despite the fact he was a tidy player, and he didn't figure much that season, but despite our differences I think he liked me and I played a lot."

The start for Souness wasn't encouraging.

"I remember Jack playing me at left-back in a pre-season friendly game at York and somewhere in Scotland." Now the one thing I am not is a left-back.

"I hated it, didn't start the season and only came in because Brian Taylor was injured in a game early on. Willie Maddren dropped into the back four and I played in midfield."

Souness siezed his chance. He became part of one of the most influential and talented midfields which the club had ever known.

His brief was to get the ball out to John Hickton. He would barnstorm his way through, then Alan Foggon would arrive late and score. That was the plan and more often than not it worked. But it depended on good delivery from Souness, David Armstrong and later Bobby Murdoch.

"Bobby had a huge influence on me," admits Souness. "Being Scottish, I knew all about Bobby. He helped me a lot, on and off the park. He had done the lot, he was a great player, and here I was playing alongside him.

"Like all great players, he had a great first touch and could pass a ball brilliantly. But he had a steelyness which wasn't obvious. He hated being beaten and could handle himself very well if the game took a physical turn.

"People don't normally associate Bobby with that type of game, but it was there if it needed to be. Before he came, I thought you only had to play when you had the ball. I was pretty good with it, but did nothing off it. He and Jack changed my attitude to the game 100 per cent."

It didn't take the 20 year old Scot long to realise that when Charlton laid down the law, you listened, and listened hard.

Graeme said: "Some players couldn't live with the way he approached the game. He always used to say that a player is only as good as his last game. I've never forgotten that. I learned everything from Jack Charlton. Wherever I have played, or managed, I have always applied the same principles which I learned with him. Without question Jack had the biggest influence on my footballing career."

It was a career, in the early days with Boro, which was mixed with all kinds of emotions. Souness liked the ladies, one or two thought that was problem, but Jack had a word, was assured about the Scot's behaviour, and it was never an issue from very early on.

On the field he needed guidance. Sent-off at Carlisle, Souness was the only Boro player to walk that season.

"I remember hitting Stan Ternent. He and I had been having a go for a while and I clipped him. I deserved to be sent off and let's just say I was told, by Jack, in no uncertain terms, that I would do no such thing again!"

One game stands out above all others from that season with Souness - the championship winning match at Luton at the end of March.

"I know a lot of the lads go on about the West Brom and Fulham matches, but that game at Luton said it all for me. They were second in the table, yet we went down there, beat them and showed how good we really were. That game, for me, emphasised just how good we were that season."

Souness earned an Under-23 cap with Scotland during the 73-74 season, playing at St James' Park against an England side which included David Mills and Willie Maddren, but by the time the call-up came, Souness had learned not to get carried away.

"I was only wheeled in because I was local and could get to the game quickly when someone got injured. I was surprised and delighted when I was called into the 30 originally chosen for the Scottish World Cup squad, but I knew I would not make it to Munich."

International honours were to follow, but not that season.

"I enjoyed it all, the ups and downs, not that there were many downs. I still have very fond memories of my time in Middlesbrough, they were great times. I was living in Chipchase Road with a landlady called Phoebe Hay, only she wasn't like a landlady, she was more like a mother to me. She helped me settle into Middlesbrough.

"Millwall and Oxford wanted to sign me when Bill Nicholson sold me from Spurs. I wasn't happy down there. I thought I could play a bit and should be in their first team. Bill thought otherwise and wanted to sell me to a club as far away from London as possible, just in case I came good and embarrassed him!"

He added: "It was closer to home for me, being from Edinburgh, but Middlesbrough became my home and I'll never forget what I learned there, on and off the field."

CHAPTER EIGHT

JANUARY

– NEWS UPDATE –

Cup run starts at Grantham

BORO'S assistant manager Harold Shepherdson had watched Grantham in a Southern League game against Dartford the previous Saturday, coming back with a simple observation: "We've only got to play like our normal form and we're into the next round. I wasn't impressed with what I saw."

Captain Stuart Boam (right) added his thoughts by saying: "We are nicely placed at the top of the table so we can relax in the Cup and possibly turn it on. We don't want any replays. The pressure is off us and maybe we can show them what we can do. We should have put six past Palace, so we are in good heart."

Unlike other teams, most notably Orient, who won 2-0 at Bristol City to close the gap at the top, and Luton, who lost 2-0 at Carlisle, Boro had not played on New Year's Day. So they were fresh enough for this Cuptie.

Jack Charlton missed the build up to the game, suffering with 'flu, and he made a decision to travel only on the morning of the game.

Coach Ian MacFarlane sent the team into the game with a simple message: "Don't get too cocky. You will have to work for everything you get."

Grantham centre-half Ron Harrison passed a late fitness test after missing the Christmas matches against Margate and Nuneaton, with the club's manager, Terry Bly, saying: "Our biggest problem is being over enthusiastic. We may try to play the game too quickly. But we are confident that given the right breaks we can beat Middlesbrough. But we must not give anything away."

Boro returned 1,200 tickets for the tie. There was a lack of petrol nationwide and only one train to Grantham, which was scheduled to arrive at 1.32pm. The kick-off was at 2pm.

Even so, the traffic and crowd congestion on what was Grantham's market day, was expected to be the worst ever.

David Armstrong's goal finally subdued a spirited performance by Southern League outfit Grantham.

Match Report

IT was only the second time in the club's history that Boro had met non-league opposition in the FA Cup and the first time since the 1913-14 season, when they beat Goole 9-3.

Despite the fact that Boro had returned 1,200 tickets. the attendance was still a ground record for a Cuptie, beating the 6,394 who watched a game against Oldham in 1967.

Jim Platt was in action early on as Grantham started brightly at their compact three-sided London Road ground, which shared its facilities with the local cricket team.

Brent Horobin pressed Frank Spraggon on the half-way line, a back pass from the left-back wasn't cleanly struck and Platt had to be smart to clear.

Brilliant footwork from Horobin saw him work his way through and send over a good cross which John Craggs gratefully cleared for a corner.

Boro settled and David Mills had a shot cleared off the line by right-back Jimmy Bloomer, but there was no stopping Boro's opener on 24 minutes.

A foul on John Hickton brought Boro a free-kick. Stuart Boam played the ball to David Armstrong, and he in turn played inside to Alan Foggon, who swept into the area and crossed for Mills to score from close range.

On the balance of play, Grantham could consider themselves unlucky, although Boro had created the more clear cut chances. But it was fair to say that the home side had created Boro more problems than most Second Division sides had done that season.

Platt saved well from Denis Benskin at the start of the second half, while Ernie Nixon headed wide. Boro settled into a patient style of play and began to create chances of their own.

Just after centre-half Ron Harrison had headed inches over, Boro went two-up and sealed the game. Foggon had broken away on the right as the home side pressed, delivering a fine cross to David Armstrong, who brought the ball under control, picked his spot and dispatched a shot into the far corner after 72 minutes.

"I must pay tribute to Grantham," said Charlton, adding: "I don't want to meet another non-league side for a long, long time."

Charlton's wish was granted in round four, when Boro were drawn away to Third Division Wrexham, who had beaten Crystal Palace in round three.

SATURDAY JANUARY 5

Grantham 0   Middlesbrough 2

Scorers: Mills 24, Armstrong 72.

Attendance: 6,573.

Collectors' Item

```
            F.A. CUP  (3rd Round Proper)


        G R A N T H A M      v    M I D D L E S B R O U G H

    Chris GARDINER          1      Jim PLATT
    Jimmy BLOOMER           2      John CRAGGS
    Andy CRAWFORD           3      Frank SPRAGGON
    Colin THOMPSON          4      Graeme SOUNESS
    Ron HARRISON            5      Stuart BOAM
    Mick CHAMBERS           6      Willie MADDREN
    Brent HOROBIN           7      Bobbie MURDOCH
    Gerry TAYLOR            8      David MILLS
    Ernie NIXON             9      John HICKTON
    Bob NORRIS             10      Alan FOGGON
    Denis BENSKIN          11      David ARMSTRONG
    Graham CLAPHAM         12      Malcolm SMITH

    REFEREE:    H. Davey        (Nottingham)
    LINESMEN:   K.C. Thorpe     (Worksop)
                R.E. Mees       (Derby)

    Any team changes will be announced before the start
    of the match.

    It is with very grateful thanks that we acknowledge that
    the balls for today's Cup-tie have been donated by:-

            John Lee and Son (Grantham) Ltd.
                         and
            Harrowby Bingo Club
```

An original team sheet for Boro's third round FA cuptie at Grantham.
It was only the second time in the club's history that they had been drawn against non-league opposition.

*The only change was that Peter Brine replaced Malcolm Smith as Boro's substitute.

– NEWS UPDATE –

Never on a Sunday

SUNDAY football was being suggested right around the country in a bid to get the crowds back to the game.

There was a feeling that kicking off at 2pm on a Saturday was affecting attendances and one way around this problem was to play a day later. A few clubs had tried it and reported that the experiment was successful, but Boro were having none of it.

Chairman Charles Amer said: "Saturday is a soccer day. Sunday is a family day, for cars and going to the seaside. The women aren't going to stand and see their menfolk going to matches on a Sunday.

"The Police have enough to do six days a week without being called upon on a Sunday as well. It may inevitably come, but the time is not right."

Those views were not shared by Charlton, who said: "Football clubs are there to entertain the crowds. If the crowds want to be entertained on a Sunday then it is up to us to do so.

"The crowds at Sunday matches so far have been promising, but this season I think we should keep on going as we are, with clubs being allowed to make up their own mind."

The MP for West Lothian, Tam Dalyell, wrote to the Home Secretary, Robert Carr, suggesting legislation to allow Sunday football, as long as it was at least four hours after church time.

* * * * *

Car deal

JOHN Craggs announced a deal with Martins of Church Road, Stockton. Boro's right-back was to join their sales promotion team, and a different brand new Datsun car would be provided every two or three months free of charge.

The cars all had one thing in common, they all had a picture of Craggs on the side.

General manager, Mr E Pick, said: "This is done with the blessing of Middlesbrough Football Club. John is a neighbour of mine and this sort of thing is nothing new."

* * * * *

Held by Villa

PRIOR to Boro's next game, away to Aston Villa, the government announced a lifting of the ban on the use of generators for floodlights for outdoor sport.

Boro were not really affected. Kick-off against Portsmouth, their next home game, had been set at 2pm and by the time they played at home again after that, the nights would be light enough to kick-off at 3pm.

It was good news for the local greyhound stadium, which had enough fuel to last until the light nights, having a 300 gallon tank, of which it used only ten gallons a night.

Charlton recalled the meeting between Boro and Villa at Ayresome Park earlier in the season, saying: "They never set up one attack. They've dropped down the table since then (now mid-table) and it's up to us to make sure they drop a bit further."

Villa had gone nine league games without a win, collecting three points and scoring three goals in the process, though they were still unbeaten at home and were at full strength for the first time in ten games.

Boro, still unbeaten away, were warned by Charlton: "This could be our toughest away game of the season. They have players like Bruce Rioch who can settle a game in a split second."

* * * * *

John Craggs joined the sales team of a local car dealership with the blessing of Middlesbrough FC.

SATURDAY JANUARY 12
Aston Villa 1   Middlesbrough 1

ASTON VILLA	**MIDDLESBROUGH**
Cumbes	Platt
Gidman	Craggs
Aitken	Spraggon
Rioch	Souness
Nicholl	Boam
Ross	Maddren
Graydon	Murdoch
Vowden (Evans 70)	Mills
Morgan	Hickton (Brine 71)
Hamilton	Foggon
Little	Armstrong

Scorers: Craggs 55, Rioch 90.

Attendance: 26,906.

Bruce Rioch, who was later to rejuvenate the Boro after liquidation in 1986, scored a last minute leveller to deny Big Jack's team victory at Villa Park.

Match Report

THERE were gasps on the terraces at Villa Park as the teams were announced and Geoff Vowden was favoured ahead of hero Trevor Hockey, who was fit again after missing the last two matches.

Boro featured on BBC TV's Match Of The Day for the first time this season, although the game was no advert for the Second Division.

Jim Platt was soon in action as Villa pressed, Ray Graydon shooting through a crowd of players, and Platt, seeing the ball late, grabbed it at the second attempt. Boro gradually got into their stride, but Bruce Rioch almost snapped them out of it when hitting a left footed shot just wide.

Alan Foggon beat his marker to set a Boro move going, taking the ball along the goal line and crossing into the area, but no-one was up in support.

Boro's passing lacked its usual accuracy and it's fair to say they had an off day. Villa were not much better and a move involving Rioch, Vowden and John Gidman came to an abrupt halt with the intervention of John Craggs, while Foggon stumbled on the ball when preparing to shoot after beating two players approaching the edge of the penalty area.

However, it was Boro who took the lead. Ten minutes into the second half Foggon broke through and was brought down by Rioch. Craggs stepped up to take the free-kick and beat the wall with a shot from 25 yards.

Mills hit the side netting late in the game while Villa substitute Alun Evans mis-kicked in front of goal and was booed by the crowd. In the final minute a drive by Rioch from the edge of the penalty area took a deflection and whistled past Platt for Villa's equaliser.

"You don't know how that goal might affect us at the end of the season," stormed Charlton. "We may live to regret it."

As it was Boro hadn't lost any ground as Orient drew 1-1 at Blackpool.

Meanwhile there was mixed news for Willie Maddren after the game. He was to be included in another England Under-23 squad, but he was destined to be substitute as Ipswich Town's Kevin Beattie was handed the coveted No. 6 shirt.

"I'm delighted. There is no better back four player in the league than Willie," enthused Charlton. "He deserves to be called up. In fact he deserves to play."

– MAN OF THE MATCH –

VILLA manager Vic Crowe chose ALAN FOGGON, reasoning: "He put in a lot of courageous running and took on my defence well."

– NEWS UPDATE –

Pompey chimes silenced

IN form Portsmouth provided Boro's only opposition at Ayresome in January. They had lost just one of their last eight matches since signing Paul Went from Fulham for £155,000 and Malcom Hanley from Leicester for £55,000. Only five of the team which lost to Boro on the opening game of the season had survived.

Portsmouth arrived at Ayresome knowing though that they had lost their previous ten visits to the stadium, but manager John Mortimore was in bullish mood, saying he thought his full strength, £500,000 team, could stop Boro's run.

He said: "We had a very similar record at Carlisle, but we went up there and turned them over this season. What we can do on one bogy ground we can do on another."

Charlton warned Boro that this would be a tough game, saying: "Portsmouth are a side who have a lot of good players on their books and who have picked up really well in the last month or so."

Pompey included an interesting player in their starting line up. Left winger Mick Mellows, now 25 years old, had been capped 16 times by England as an amateur. He had asked Portsmouth for a trial, they liked what they saw and Mellows gave up his teaching job to turn full time pro.

*   *   *   *   *

SATURDAY JANUARY 19

Middlesbrough 3   Portsmouth 0

MIDDLESBROUGH	PORTSMOUTH
Platt	Milkins
Craggs	Roberts
Spraggon	Hand
Souness	Piper
Boam	Went
Maddren	Manley
Murdoch	Marinello
Mills	Kellard
Hickton (Smith 72)	Davies
Foggon	Reynolds
Armstrong	Mellows
	Sub: Lewis

Scorers: Foggon 49, Smith 74, Souness 76.

Attendance: 21,774.

Match Report

PORTSMOUTH goalkeeper John Milkins had made more than 400 appearances for the club when he arrived at Ayresome and he was thrust straight into action, making a brilliant save when clawing away a Willie Maddren header from under the crossbar in the third minute.

Boro continued to press and John Craggs flashed a shot just wide before beating two men and having another shot deflected for a corner.

Two penalty appeals were turned down in quick succession as a Hickton cross appeared to be controlled with a hand and then the same player was sent sprawling under a heavy challenge.

The best chance of the opening 45 minutes fell, however, to Portsmouth. Jim Platt and Maddren went up for the same ball which dropped at the feet of Ron Davies who, just two or three yards out, spooned it over the bar.

Boro eventually made the breakthrough four minutes into the second half. Stuart Boam headed a Bobby Murdoch corner on to Alan Foggon, who swept the ball into the net.

David Mills should have made it two a minute later but hit his shot straight at Milkins.

Two goals in as many minutes gave the scoreline a more realistic look. Malcolm Smith had replaced John Hickton after 72 minutes, and two minutes later he was on the scoresheet as a cross from Frank Spraggon was only half cleared and Smith hammered it home with virtually his first touch.

Boro, dominant throughout, had the bit between their teeth now and scored a third after 76 minutes. Craggs, who had enjoyed an outstanding game, coasted down Boro's right flank and crossed for Graeme Souness, who rifled in his second goal of the season with a first time shot.

"Young Malcolm Smith comes on full of enthusiasm, challenging for everything, but to expect him to do that for 90 minutes would be asking a lot," said Charlton, explaining the use of a tactical substitute.

"John Hickton takes the steam out of the opposition. He can give it everything knowing he will be off for the last 15 minutes. When you have 12 good players, use them!"

Pompey boss John Mortimore said: "I can see nothing stopping Middlesbrough now. They are a team in every sense of the word."

Orient had kept up the pressure with a 2-1 home win over Sunderland, but Boro were now ten points clear of the fourth placed team.

– MAN OF THE MATCH –

A three way tie, according to Portsmouth manager John Mortimore. ALAN FOGGON: "Determined front running and vital first goal." GRAEME SOUNESS: "Superb midfield contribution." JOHN CRAGGS: "Outstanding work in defence and on overlap."

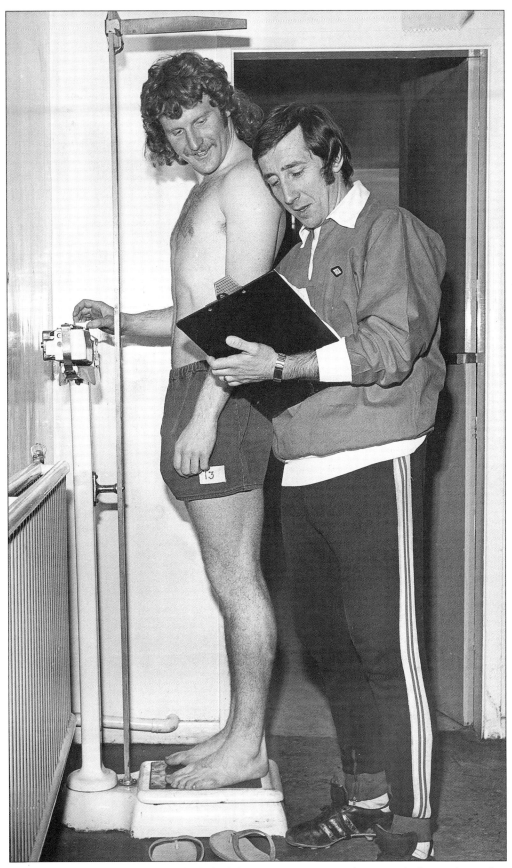

Malcolm Smith, here receiving a medical check from trainer Jimmy Headrige, "weighed in" with a goal against Portsmouth at Ayresome Park.

– NEWS UPDATE –

Cup run wrecked at Wrexham

THE Wrexham manager John Neal had his build up plans to the FA Cup fourth round tie shattered by tiny Welsh League club Blaenau Ffestiniog.

Third Division Wrexham had planned to go to Blackpool for a few days to get away from the tension but they were forced to stay in Wales because Blaenau Ffestiniog insisted on playing a previously postponed Welsh Cuptie three days before Boro's visit. Wrexham duly dispatched the minnows by 6-3, but it was still a hard game which they felt they could have done without.It was the second time that Wrexham had conceded three goals in five days, having done the same against Walsall the previous Saturday, and Neal said: "This has disrupted all our preparations. I am not able to say what I am thinking."

Future Ayresome Park manager, John Neal, masterminded Boro's FA Cup exit when Wrexham scored the only goal on a waterlogged Racecourse Ground in January.

Boro had been called in for extra training with Ian McFarlane saying: "I think that the team has benefitted from putting in a bit of extra work. It has helped us to focus our minds. Our attitude has to be the same for this game as any other."

As for Charlton, he had changed his tune from the start of the season, saying: "Earlier in the campaign I thought a Cup run would interfere with our main aim, promotion, but now I think we can take it all in our stride. We are starting to awaken the people of Middlesbrough and a good Cup run would help."

*   *   *   *   *

SATURDAY JANUARY 26

Wrexham 1   Middlesbrough 0

WREXHAM	MIDDLESBROUGH
Lloyd	Platt
Jones	Craggs
Fogg	Spraggon
Evans	Souness
May	Boam
Whittle	Maddren
Tinnion	Murdoch
Sutton	Mills
Davies	Hickton (Smith 58)
Smallman	Foggon
Griffiths	Armstrong
Sub: Thomas	

Scorer: Smallman 38.

Attendance: 20,612.

Match Report

WREXHAM were the first team to understand how Middlesbrough played that season.

The tactic of using Alan Foggon as a runner from midfield, moving on to through balls from Bobby Murdoch, David Armstrong and Graeme Souness, didn't work as Wrexham simply kept enough men back behind the ball. Lashing rain and a mudbath of a pitch didn't help Boro's game either.

Boro applied early pressure, but passes were going astray in the quagmire and Wrexham soon sensed they would be in with a chance. David Smallman had a shot blocked before Boro created a chance which should have been taken, David Mills heading a John Craggs cross just wide with goalkeeper Brian Lloyd struggling in the mud.

A snap shot from centre-half Eddie May went just past the post, while Frank Spraggon headed off the line as Boro were temporarily down to ten men as Willie Maddren had been taken off, bleeding heavily from a head wound.

The only goal of the game came in the 38th minute. Boro only half cleared a corner and Smallman blasted the ball into the roof of the net.

Boro were backed by a healthy support, including several members of the Green Howards who were based in nearby Chester, after spending three years in Osnabruk.

But there was precious little to cheer for any Boro fans, though the team did pick up their game in the second half with Mills flashing a shot narrowly wide. Stuart Boam was just wide from a corner, while Lloyd had to be smart to deny Malcolm Smith, who had replaced John Hickton after only six minutes of the second half.

It was almost impossible for players to keep their feet in the conditions, but Wrexham managed well enough and Jim Platt had to tip a Geoff Davies header over the bar. Late in the game, Smith intercepted a back-pass but he hurriedly shot wide.

"We went there to try and win, it wasn't a case of having promotion on our minds," said captain Stuart Boam.

"You can't beat a bit of glamour and we wanted some, but we didn't have any luck that was going. On the day Wrexham deserved to go through."

It was Boro's first away defeat of the season and the first time they had failed to score in 17 matches.

– MAN OF THE MATCH –

IN the absence of John Neal, the choice was made by a concensus of local Welsh journalists and the unanimous choice was DAVID MILLS: "Ever dangerous" and "The player who always looked likely to earn Middlesbrough a replay".

REFLECTIONS

Bobby Murdoch

THE signing who made all the difference, perhaps in more ways than one.

Robert White Murdoch, or Bobby to his friends, was the only major signing made by Jack Charlton in his first year in charge at Ayresome.

But what a signing. Here was a player who had seen it and done it, more than once, at the highest level.

Born towards the end of the Second World War near Glasgow, he had represented his country, won a European Cup with Glasgow Celtic, as well as League Championships and domestic cups with the club he had joined as a boy.

A number of factors came into play with regard to his move to Middlesbrough.

The over-riding factor was that Murdoch wasn't a regular in the Celtic side any more. He had appeared in the reserves that season while younger players came through, but added to that was the fact that he wanted to play in England.

Bobby said: "For all I had been lucky in my career, I still felt as though something was missing. I needed to test myself in the English League. I wanted to see how good I was there and what standard of football was being played south of the Border."

The answer to that was perhaps predictable. Murdoch exuded class. He couldn't run far, but no-one was his superior when passing the ball.

"The game was a wee bit fast at first, but I quickly adapted. I was lucky in that I could hit a ball where it was supposed to go and there were players at Middlesbrough who could make the best of it."

Murdoch was a product of the Jock Stein academy and it was the friendship between the Celtic supremo and Jack Charlton which was the major contributory factor in his move south.

"I had played against Jack in his testimonial game at Elland Road the day before Charlton took over at Ayresome," he explains. "I had also scored past him in a European Cuptie three years earlier!

"I know there was a lot of respect between the two managers, but I don't think anything was set up that night."

A huge crowd of 34,963 watched Leeds play Celtic in that testimonial, and 24 hours later Charlton was at Ayresome, to be followed in the middle of September by Murdoch.

Bobby watched the first game played after he joined, a goalless draw at Orient on a Monday night, before making his debut the following Saturday in another goalless draw at Blackpool.

His home debut, a week later, was crowned with the first of five goals that season, and was the opener in a 2-0 win over Bristol City.

Murdoch is credited by most people as bringing the best out of Graeme Souness, a 20 year old who had, by his own admission, a big opinion of himself.

"He thought he should have been in the Spurs team ahead of Dave Mackay," reflects Murdoch.

"He was a bit headstrong, a bit of a Jack The Lad figure. I had been brought down to help the youngsters through, as well as playing my own game, and I took Graeme under my wing in a way.

"He had trained with Celtic when he was a schoolboy and I remembered him from then. But he listened to me, or at least he seemed to! He was a fine player, he just needed direction and I think we got there in the end.

"We had some fine youngsters and in David Armstrong had a great passer of the ball with his left foot. But everyone played a part."

Murdoch seldom mixed with the players socially, but that was out of commitment to his family, not any high handed attitude against players who had not achieved anywhere near as much.

"There was never any of that at the club. No-one got above their station. There was a respect for each other, a healthy respect for what one could do for the team. You can't win a game on your own.

"I was older than most, in fact all of them. I had family and we used to go out for a meal on a Saturday night, maybe to the Tontine if we were wanting to head out of town. It was OK in town as well. It wasn't like Glasgow where I had to be careful where I was going in case I went into Rangers territory!

"But I preferred a quiet life away from the game."

On the field his expertise guided Boro through sticky patches, not that you would need a second hand to count the number of occasions they occurred.

"We had one instruction which over-rode all the others, that was to make sure we played to the highest standards possible.

"A lot of people thought we were a defensive team, but how could that be? We had a good defence which played to the highest standards it could, and likewise up front, while the game was largely run through us in midfield.

"I had come from a team which won everything to a team which was winning everything. I had a great time. A lot of people wondered how I would adapt to playing in front of much smaller crowds. I had been used to 50,000-plus at Parkhead, but that was never a problem.

"When you are on a field you can hear the occasional comment, but by and large you just concentrate on your own game and when it is going as well as it was then, you don't get too many individual comments from small crowds anyway.

"Ayresome Park was a great place to play, the surface was excellent and if you couldn't play on that and please the fans then you couldn't play anywhere."

Modesty could have been Murdoch's middle name. He allowed his football to do the talking and Boro fans were privileged to see the Bothwell brogue turned into Ayresome eloquence.

CHAPTER NINE
FEBRUARY

– NEWS UPDATE –

Bonus for Souness

IN the week leading up the game at Nottingham Forest, Graeme Souness had a booking overturned and therefore avoided his second suspension of the season. The booking rescinded was one received at Grantham and their manager, Terry Bly, spoke up for Souness at an FA hearing.

"I was very impressed with the way the FA handled it," said Charlton. "Irrespective of whether it was Graeme or not. It was good of Terry to speak up for us and we're obviously delighted that there will be no suspension."

That same week saw Charlton write to the FA supporting Forest player Liam O'Kane, who had been sent-off when playing against Boro at Ayresome Park.

Forest still had their problems, however. Former captain, 29 year old Peter Hindley, refused to play for the club.

He explained why, saying: "I feel the club are stringing me along. They are keeping me here just in case there are injuries to other players and I am refusing to play for the first team again."

Forest manager Alan Brown said in reply: "If he refuses to play, he can't expect wages from us."

Hindley was placed on the transfer list.

Brown was still in upbeat mood when assessing the chances of his side against Boro.

"This is the best time to get at Boro, when they have been on the wrong end of a Cup shock. We had a good Cup win over First Division Manchester City (4-1) and we see this Saturday's game as a great chance to start a big promotion drive.

Meanwhile Charlton denied reports he was to make a move for Pop Robson, who was unsettled at West Ham.

Captain Stuart Boam had his opinions on the possibility of new players, saying: "Obviously any manager is on the lookout for good players who become available, but how many of those are there?

"At the beginning of the season the supporters were telling the club to buy, but Jack had confidence in the players he inherited and said he would give them three months to show what they could do. He has stood by his word and the lads appreciate the fact he has confidence in them."

As for Charlton, he championed the club's youth policy. "It's working well. Players like Maddren, Armstrong, Smith, Brine and Mills have all come through and are now worth a lot of money on the transfer market."

* * * * *

SATURDAY FEBRUARY 2
Nottingham Forest 5   Middlesbrough 1

NOTTINGHAM FOREST	MIDDLESBROUGH
Barron	Platt
O'Kane	Craggs
Winfield	Spraggon
Chapman	Souness
Cottam	Boam
Richardson	Maddren
McKenzie	Murdoch
Lyall	Mills
Martin	Hickton (Smith 52)
Jackson	Foggon
Bowyer	Armstrong
Sub: Serella	

Scorers: Bowyer 8, Winfield 19, Foggon 24, Martin 30, Lyall 82, Lyall pen 86.

Attendance: 18,799.

An early goal scored by Forest forward, Ian Bowyer (above), was instrumental in halting Boro's 25 match unbeaten league run which came to an abrupt end with a thumping 5-1 defeat at the City Ground.

Match Report

BORO lost their unbeaten league away record in spectacular style. It was to be their first defeat in 25 matches, and the first time anyone had got the better of them since Fulham on September 1.

They didn't lose too much ground though, as second placed Orient lost 3-0 at Carlisle, while Luton won 1-0 at Villa.

It was Boro who made the brighter start, almost scoring with the first attack of the game.

David Armstrong combined with Graeme Souness to set up a chance for David Mills but he shot into the side netting.

It took just eight minutes for Forest to find the back of the net. The speed of the move had Boro reeling as Duncan McKenzie rounded off a lightning quick break to cross into the area and all Ian Bowyer had to do was to tap into the net from close range.

Willie Maddren had a goal disallowed minutes later, but there was no stopping Forest's second after 19 minutes. Jim Platt conceded a corner and punched the flag kick straight to John Winfield. The left-back chested it down and flashed a shot into the bottom corner.

Boro pulled one back five minutes later. A John Craggs free kick was deflected to Boam, his shot was blocked, but Alan Foggon reacted quicker than anyone else to head into the roof of the net.

Any thoughts Boro had of getting back into the game were extinguished after half an hour when Souness conceded a free kick with an over-eager tackle and Neil Martin lashed an unstoppable shot beyond Platt.

Boro, although better in the second half, were well and truly beaten by a side which had everything going for it on the day.

Malcolm Smith had replaced John Hickton a minute before he almost pulled a goal back on 53 minutes, drawing 'keeper Jim Barron, but running the ball out of play.

A Craggs free-kick was punched clear, Mills went close and Craggs went close again as Boro pressed, but Forest, who had a Bowyer goal disallowed, scored two in four of the last ten minutes.

Breaking quickly from a Boro attack, Bowyer crossed from the left and George Lyall headed in a simple goal. Lyall's second and Forest's fifth came from the penalty spot four minutes from time."

"We feel unbelievably sick," said captain Stuart Boam after the game.

"But we also feel sorry for Blackpool. We'll have to take it out on them on Saturday. It's a long time since we took a beating like that, it has really brought us down to earth.

"We have no excuses, no alibis, no complaints or grouses, we were turned over and are grimly determined to put it right. I can imagine what the fans are thinking. Boro have gone great guns like this before and then slumped, but I don't think that will happen this time."

Charlton agreed, saying: "The lads can't perform as well as they have done and then die. They were destroyed by two sensational goals which wouldn't be scored in 30 attempts. It's back to hard work on the training field."

A famous name in the Teesside travel industry, Bee-Line, supplied the official coach to Middlesbrough FC during the 1973-74 season.

Charlton staying on Teesside says Amer

PRESS speculation that Jack Charlton was to join Newcastle incensed chairman Charles Amer.

"A shake of the hand and the word of Jack Charlton is better to me than a load of contracts. It would be an insult to offer our manager a contract at this stage because it would be tantamount to doubting his integrity.

"If Jack wanted a contract he would come and ask for one and he would automatically get it. The people of Teesside have been noted for generations as being among the hardest in the country to please and always demanding the best. But I have found that if you play fair with them and prove you are doing your best, they might be slow to appreciate you, but once they are with you they are with you all the way and our fans appreciate what is being done here."

Charlton was equally annoyed about the speculation, saying: "I'm tired of telling people that I didn't come to Middlesbrough for the money. I came because of the club's potential. I am not going to make a success and then jump off the bandwagon. I have proved nothing yet.

"This sort of thing causes upsets and friction in the game where there is no right to be any. I'll be frightened to go to Newcastle to watch a game in case it causes more comments!"

* * * * *

Three without a win

BORO were just six short of their full tally of points from the previous season and were moving well, but not well enough, according to the powers that be. The team trained in snow, sleet and driving rain without a day off in the week leading to a game against a Blackpool team which had improved sufficiently to move to fifth in the table, following a run of ten Second Division games without defeat.

Blackpool's manager, Harry Potts, was in confident mood, saying: "I know Boro had a setback at Forest, but they are still in a very strong position. I think the three games over the Easter period will determine who goes up with them.

"But we are improving, playing quite well and beginning to play with confidence and we're looking forward to this one."

As for Charlton, his assessment of the forthcoming task was: "I hope we play the way we are capable of playing, in which case we could get an easy result."

* * * * *

Lucky escape

Charlton's coach, Ian MacFarlane, had a lucky escape ahead of the game as he explained: "I was about four miles this side of Wetherby on the way to watch Manchester City and Derby when a tyre on a 20 ton tanker blew and the huge outer rim smashed into the front of my car.

"There was a lot of damage, but everyone was OK. I went to the tanker to get the insurance details but, on the way back to my car, another lorry smashed into it! It couldn't have been much closer."

* * * * *

Boro's chief coach, Ian MacFarlane, had a lucky escape when his parked car was struck by a lorry on the A1 near Wetherby.

SATURDAY FEBRUARY 9

Middlesbrough 0	Blackpool 0
MIDDLESBROUGH	**BLACKPOOL**
Platt	Burridge
Craggs	Curtis
Spraggon	Harrison
Souness	Alcock
Boam	James
Maddren	Suddaby
Murdoch (Smith 48)	Burns
Mills	Suddick
Hickton	Dyson
Foggon	Bentley
Armstrong	Ainscow
	Sub: McEwan

Attendance: 21,913.

Match Report

THERE were only two games played in the Second Division that day as wind and a considerable amount of rain swept across the country.

Notts County beat Portsmouth at Meadow Lane, but there wasn't a goal in sight at Ayresome where conditions were far from perfect, but playable.

Both teams went for it from the off and Glyn James had to hammer a backpass to John Burridge under pressure from John Hickton. John Craggs then sent Hickton away, with left-back Steve Harrison intervening.

Boro settled into their stride and a spectacular run from Craggs took him more than half the length of the field before he was brought down by inside-left Bill Bentley. Graeme Souness had a shot blocked and Boro had appeals for a penalty turned down when Hickton appeared to be upended by left-half Peter Suddaby.

David Armstrong was brought down in the box minutes later, and again no penalty was given. Boro were completely dominant but could not find a way through. Burridge was finally beaten by a close range shot from Armstrong, but right-half Terry Alcock cleared off the line. Alan Foggon had a goal disallowed and Armstrong another shot cleared off the line.

Boro lost Bobby Murdoch in the early stages of the second half, but such was their dominance that Jim Platt did not touch the ball for 19 minutes - and then it was to collect a backpass!

David Mills rode three tackles to set up Souness, whose shot was blocked. Foggon shot wide when he should have scored, and then shot over, while Burridge saved at the feet of Hickton.

Burridge was beaten minutes later, John Curtis clearing of the line this time, and Boro, with Platt reckoning he had touched the ball five times all match, had to settle for a draw.

"Everyone at the game must have been satisfied," was the surprising reaction from Charlton, who continued: "The lads went from the first whistle to the last without a let up. It spoke volumes for their fitness that they were going harder at the end than the beginning!

"It also spoke volumes for their dedication and character. They just didn't want to lose. The fans must be sick at dropping a point, but imagine how the players feel."

Blackpool manager Harry Potts admitted: "It was not our intention to play so defensively. You have to give credit to Middlesbrough for the way they played. I think they played really, really well, but our defence was magnificent."

That defence had helped Blackpool stretch their unbeaten run to 11 games.

– MAN OF THE MATCH –

HARRY Potts nominated GRAEME SOUNESS, reasoning: "He did a lot of good work in midfield and laid the ball off well."

A rather flattering caricature of the skipper and Big John drawn by Pat Adams. Surely they were never as good looking as that?

Graeme Souness gave an impressive midfield performance against Blackpool.

– NEWS UPDATE –

Tempting Bonus

IT had been revealed that Boro's players were on a £2,000 a man promotion bonus before they next took the field.

But no-one seemed to bother about the money, certainly off the field, as Boro's fans were sensing that a return to the First Division, after a 20 year absence, was just around the corner.

*   *   *   *   *

The drawing of tigers' teeth

BORO had injury worries throughout the week ahead of their next game at Boothferry Park against Hull City.

Bobby Murdoch was struggling with a knee ligament injury picked up against Blackpool and was ruled out of the trip to Humberside as early as the Wednesday before the game. However David Mills (hamstring), David Armstrong (badly bruised foot) and John Hickton (bruised shins), were passed fit to play, with Peter Brine taking the place of Murdoch.

City had switched a midweek reserve game against Lincoln to Goole to prevent the pitch cutting up, while they were to include a 20 year old amateur in their side. Midfield player John Hawley, who was very highly rated, preferred to remain within his family's antiques business, rather than turn professional.

City were without experienced right-back Frank Banks, who had previously missed only half a dozen games in the last four years, suffering with strained ankle ligaments.

Ahead of the game Charlton said: "If the lads show the same determination as they did last week, we have no fears at all. This is pretty well a local derby with not a lot of love lost, so I am looking forward to a hard, competitive game."

*   *   *   *   *

SATURDAY FEBRUARY 16

Hull City 1   Middlesbrough 3

HULL CITY	MIDDLESBROUGH
Wealands	Platt
McGill	Craggs
De Vries	Spraggon
Burnett	Souness
Deere	Boam
Blampey	Maddren (Gates 76)
Hawley	Brine
Lord	Mills
Pearson	Hickton
Wagstaff	Foggon
Greenwood	Armstrong
Sub: O'Riley	

Scorers: Hickton 7, Mills 35, Foggon 51, Pearson 81.

Attendance: 15,287.

Match Report

HULL City were the only Second Division team unbeaten at home, until Boro arrived.

Boro should have had a penalty when John Hawley brought down David Armstrong after just two minutes. Nothing was given, but Boro continued to pile on the pressure from the word go.

It took just seven minutes to take the lead. Alan Foggon cut in from the left, was tackled and fell to ground but, holding on to the ball, he stabbed it to the far post where John Hickton was left with a simple chance.

An excellent save from Jeff Wealands denied David Mills minutes later, with Jim Platt called into action at the other end, tipping over a Hawley cross.

The game had really opened up. Hawley went close and Boro suffered a blow when Willie Maddren was injured, but it was nothing serious. Boro were able to get back at their hosts and take a two goal lead after 35 minutes.

Graeme Souness whipped in a low ball to David Mills, the City defence hesitated, Wealands then came racing out, and Mills kept his head before lobbing over the advancing 'keeper. Minutes before half-time Boro had a 'third goal' disallowed, but were so much in control that it came as no surprise when they increased their advantage and sealed the game with a third, six minutes into the second half.

Souness again was the provider, this time to Foggon. Wealands came out again and Foggon beat him with ease.

Hull threw everything forward and Platt did well to save from Denis Burnett and Roy Greenwood. Boro lost Maddren with less than 15 minutes remaining, Bill Gates replacing the defender, who had double vision.

Five minutes later Hull reduced the arrears as Stuart Pearson powerfully headed in a right-wing corner. It was too little too late for the Tigers.

Charlton's reaction: "I was pleased with the win, but a bit disappointed with the way the lads fell away towards the end."

There was a more positive reaction from striker John Hickton who said: "I have waited a long time for promotion and now it looks as though it could be on the horizon. Saturday's goal was just my sixth of the season, but I don't mind who is scoring them."

> ### – MAN OF THE MATCH –
> *THE Hull City manager Terry Neill refused to comment after the match and the nomination was left to an experienced Hull sports writer Brian Taylor.*
> *He couldn't split ALAN FOGGON "for non stop running and a courageous performance" and GRAEME SOUNESS "for an excellent midfield display".*

*Alan Foggon coolly slots home Boro's third goal past the stranded
Hull City keeper, Jeff Wealands, in a fine 3-1 away win at Boothferry Park.*

*John Hickton scored the
first goal against Hull City
and sensed that promotion
was now a distinct
possibility.*

– NEWS UPDATE –

Squeezing past the Robins

IT was almost taken for granted that Boro would win their final game of February, at home to struggling Swindon.

The Wiltshire club would be without Welsh Under-23 international Terry Hubbard, who dislocated a shoulder in a 4-1 midweek home defeat by Notts County. Seventeen year old England youth international Dave Syrett took his place, while centre-forward Roy Compton made his debut.

It was top against bottom, with Boro taking on a side which had conceded seven goals in four days prior to playing at Ayresome. Prior to the home defeat by Notts County, Swindon had suffered a 3-0 defeat at Millwall, who also had three goals disallowed.

Swindon had taken only two points away from home all season, drawing at Orient and Preston, yet Charlton warned his team against complacency, saying: "Unless you watch these apparent underdog teams all the way, you can be struggling. Take nothing for granted and show no hint of complacency."

Boro welcomed back Bobby Murdoch, who replaced Peter Brine.

*   *   *   *   *

SATURDAY FEBRUARY 23
Middlesbrough 2   Swindon Town 1

MIDDLESBROUGH	**SWINDON TOWN**
Platt	Spratley
Craggs	McLaughlin
Spraggon	Trollope
Souness	Butler
Boam	Potter
Maddren	Stroud (Clarke 10)
Murdoch	Moss
Mills	Dixon
Hickton	Compton
Foggon	Syrett
Armstrong	Jenkins
Sub: Brine	

Scorers: Hickton 9, Foggon 46, Compton 80.

Attendance: 25,194.

Match Report

IT may have been top versus bottom, but Boro made heavy weather of their win.

Their closest pursuers, Orient, drew at home with Hull, while Blackpool kept up their good work with a 3-0 win at Notts County. Luton, with two games in hand over Blackpool, won 2-1 at home to Crystal Palace. All three were on 37 points as Boro drew nine points clear.

It was a carbon copy of the start to the game at Hull, with Boro almost going into the lead in the first minute, eventually finding the back of the net eight minutes later.

Alan Foggon set up Graeme Souness in the first minute, and his cross was perfect for David Armstrong, who wasted a clear scoring opportunity when heading wide.

The opening goal came after goalkeeper Alan Spratley, making what was just his second appearance of the season, punched clear as David Mills came racing in. Foggon just missed the ball, Armstrong had a shot blocked and the ball ran loose to Hickton, who hammered home.

Left-half Ken Stroud was taken off injured a minute later and soon after that Mills hit the post with Spratley beaten.

Boro doubled their advantage in the first minute of the second half. Bobby Murdoch sent Hickton away down Boro's right and his cross found Foggon, who shot through from close range.

Ten minutes from time Platt came out to collect a David Moss cross, but Roy Compton got there first to head a goal on his debut.

Boro had several near misses, but overall did not play very well, a point which was not lost on right-back John Craggs, who said: "You can't credit it. We played badly and won, yet we played so well against Blackpool and only drew."

Charlton, however, was quick to defend his team, saying: "We weren't all that bad you know. We were only bad in comparison to the way we have played this season. We have got to push our standards up all the time."

A safe pair of hands: Jim Platt's performance against Swindon received the plaudits of the press core.

REFLECTIONS

David Armstrong

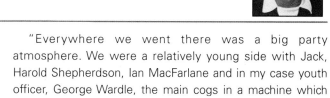

THE most naturally gifted left footed player to have been on Boro's books for years - that was a familiar description at the time which still applies today to David Armstrong.

Without doubt he was one of the best crossers of the ball in the business and few have bettered him since.

Yet Armstrong wasn't a regular in the side when Jack Charlton took over. He had made his debut as a 17 year old the season before last and while he had played a fair few games, he wasn't sure of his place.

"It was on the pre-season tour of Scotland that Jack noticed what I could do," says the player always known as 'Spike'.

"Jack had a system which he wanted to play. He had it set in his mind and I fitted into that system."

Armstrong, playing wide on the left side of midfield, was one of just three players, Stuart Boam and Willie Maddren being the others, who were ever present that season.

"They were special times," says Spike.

"It was such an enjoyable season. The biggest thing we had in our favour was the teamwork and maybe that's what made it so enjoyable. I was only a young lad trying to break through, but I was made to feel very much a part of the team and I'll never forget that.

"It was no surprise that we were a force to be reckoned with. It was all down to Jack. It was his script. He called the shots and he knew what he was doing.

"His words were simple: 'Go and enjoy it, you never know when it may come round again'. We all played with that in mind."

Charlton was thorough in his preparation. TV coverage was minimal and players would perhaps only come across each other three or four times a season. Two of those occasions would be when they were playing each other.

It wasn't a case, as it is now, of seeing just about every player every week if you know where, or have the inclination, to look.

"We were on Match Of The Day only twice that season, and any time other teams were on TV it was usually regional and not shown in too many other areas.

"So we relied a lot on the dossiers which Jack had ordered from his team of helpers. He had contacts around the country and had two or three at the club who would go and watch matches for him.

"But, while we spoke about the opposition, we didn't alter our game to suit them. We were just aware of their dangermen. It was all part of Jack's way of working and we benefitted from it.

"Everywhere we went there was a big party atmosphere. We were a relatively young side with Jack, Harold Shepherdson, Ian MacFarlane and in my case youth officer, George Wardle, the main cogs in a machine which entertained a lot of the time, but one which always knew how to win. It didn't always work, but we were never far away, except at Nottingham Forest where we lost 5-1!"

There is an interesting parallel drawn by Armstrong when he is asked to put into context just how good Boro were.

"Look at Ajax now and you see Boro of 25 years ago. It's a great pity it has taken until now for some clubs to realise that you can't buy success.

"If you're good enough you're old enough," says the man who was the youngest member of the team at the time.

"I had been a Sunderland fan all my childhood, but was impressed with Boro when I was given a chance there. It was either Boro or Manchester United and I have no regrets in making the choice I did."

There isn't one outstanding game which Spike brings to mind from that time, but he remembers the 4-0 win at Fulham as 'one in the eye for the London press!'

"According to the London scene that Fulham team was going to take us apart. No way were we going to let that happen and we gave them the biggest beating they took all season. I think then that we went close to earning the respect we deserved.

"Football is all about the fans. It is them who have kept the game going for the last 100 years and it is when people lose sight that football is an entertainment business that it will fall apart.

"It is a pity that few players who are starting at the same age that I did are now just joining the game to see what they can get out of it without putting anything in.

"At the time I was frightened to go in and ask for a £5 rise which would have taken my wages to only £20.

"But money was never an issue. We played because we enjoyed it. Mind you, one thing remains the same, it is still better to play than to train!"

Armstrong says there were not that many players who he didn't enjoy playing against, citing just two in the First Division when the side went up, simply saying: " Tommy Smith and Johnny Giles were awkward!"

Diplomacy at its best!

"We had honesty, integrity and loyalty running through our team. We respected each other for what we could do and they were special times."

CHAPTER TEN
MARCH

Revie impressed

LES Allen's scouting mission presumably was to find another job, as during the following week his side lost 2-0 at home to Luton in front of the lowest crowd in the club's history and Allen was sacked.

Luton's win put them second in the table, while elsewhere Orient were beaten at Forest.

Boro were given a vote of confidence off the pitch during the week, when Leeds United manager Don Revie, speaking at a sportsman's dinner in aid of Bill Gates at the Marton Country Club, said: "I believe you are on the threshhold of something great at Middlesbrough.

"It won't happen overnight, but you have had a wonderful start. You will get promotion to the First Division, then you've got to go for the Championship of the league and then Europe.

"I know what Jack Charlton is thinking because I felt exactly the same 12 years ago at Leeds and Jack will strive exactly the same as I have done.

"As a Middlesbrough man myself I knew Jack would do a good job here. He is a great coach with firm views on the game. I hope everyone in Middlesbrough gets behind him and the opening game of next season sees Boro playing Leeds!"

* * * * *

Teesside born Leeds manager, Don Revie, was so impressed with the Jack Charlton's Middlesbrough team that he stated in public. "I believe you are on the threshold of something great."

McAndrew honoured

TONY McAndrew was in the Scotland Youth team which won 2-1 away to Belgium in a European Youth Tournament qualifying tie first-leg game.

* * * * *

Rampant at Roker as two are sent-off

ROKER Park was the next venue for the Middlesbrough roadshow as Charlton's men took on a Sunderland side which had won three on the trot.

Sunderland manager Bob Stokoe conceded: "This will be a hell of a hard game." Charlton also conceded it would be, adding: "But we are in a position to enjoy it."

He went on: "I wish Sunderland well. I hope they are up there with us at the end of the season, but they would probably have to beat us to stand a chance of that. So it's a pressure game. The result is of great importance to the both of us."

Captain Stuart Boam went one step further, saying: "Actually it is more important for them to win. If we win they can kiss goodbye to promotion. If they win they are in with a chance."

It was a point echoed by Stokoe, who said: "If our supporters are still thinking along the lines of promotion then we'll do our best to keep the interest alive.

"But I'm not going to kid anybody. We are seven points short of the No.3 slot with 13 games to play and we would need maximum points to go up. It's next season which matters. That's when we'll have to get cracking."

* * * * *

SATURDAY MARCH 2
Sunderland 0   Middlesbrough 2

SUNDERLAND	**MIDDLESBROUGH**
Montgomery	Platt
Malone	Craggs
Bolton	Spraggon
Horswill (Longhorn 62)	Souness
Watson	Boam
Belfitt	Maddren
Kerr	Murdoch
Hughes	Mills
Halom	Hickton (Brine 66)
Porterfield	Foggon
Tueart	Armstrong

Scorers: Mills 15, Foggon 47.

Attendance: 41,658.

Match Report

AN electric atmosphere from an almost full house greeted the two teams when they took the field for the 94th Tees-Wear derby.

Boro started brightly in pursuit of their fourth league win at Roker Park. Alan Foggon was sent sprawling in the penalty area in the opening minutes, but no penalty was given.

Foggon again caused problems when breaking quickly down Boro's right, his cross falling to Bobby Murdoch, who had a shot blocked, while Boro's next attack brought a corner from which they took the lead. David Armstrong floated over a teasing flag kick and David Mills raced in to blast Boro ahead after 15 minutes.

Three minutes later Denis Tueart was booked for something he said to the referee, a booking which was later to prove significant. The home side had appeals for handball against Armstrong in the penalty area turned down, then almost equalised when Platt was beaten by a close range effort from Billy Hughes and Stuart Boam had to clear off the line.

Platt then saved from Micky Horswill, while Jimmy Montgomery dropped the ball following an Armstrong corner, smothering his error just in time.

The game erupted shortly after half-time.

Boro went two up after 47 minutes. Graeme Souness took a quick free-kick, Armstrong gained possession and slipped a good ball forward. Sunderland appealed for offside, it wasn't given and Foggon nipped in to tuck the ball past Montgomery who, seconds later, was booked for protesting.

Three minutes later Sunderland were down to nine men. Captain Bobby Kerr spoke out of turn to the referee and was immediately dismissed. Tueart, having already been booked, raced up to the official and said something else. He, too, was given his marching orders.

Two men short and two goals down, Sunderland had a mountain to climb. They brought on Dennis Longhorn, a £30,000 purchase from Mansfield, while Boro replaced John Hickton with Peter Brine.

Willie Maddren shaved a post with a good effort and Mills hit a shot straight at Montgomery as Boro completed a win which took them nine points clear at the top.

Sunderland said they were considering an appeal against the sendings off. Boro distanced themselves from the situation, with Charlton saying: "There was no way we could do anything about the sendings-off. At that stage the game could so easily have got out of hand, but my players refused to get involved.

"They showed great character and I'm proud of them. If you lose control you lose the match and that's what happened to Sunderland."

Bob Stokoe conceded that Boro were: "Without doubt the best team in the Second Division," adding: "But the decisions went against us and the game was ruined.

"The players involved behaved badly and I was very disturbed about it, but we should have had a penalty and might have scored the first goal."

It was the biggest attendance of the season which watched Boro's third double of the season.

– MAN OF THE MATCH –

GIVEN that feelings were still running high long after the game, the Man Of The Match question was posed to Hartlepool boss Len Ashurst and not Bob Stokoe. Ashurst picked DAVID MILLS, saying: "He never stopped running at Sunderland's defence in a non stop display. "He was effective up front and easy to find with the ball."

Alan Foggon leaves gasping defenders trailing in his wake, as this goal secured a league double over arch local rivals Sunderland at Roker Park.

– NEWS UPDATE –

League team nominations

TWO of Boro's players were in the Division Two side named at a PFA dinner at the Hilton Hotel in London before the club was next in action.

John Craggs and Willie Maddren (left) were the two nominated, but Charlton wasn't too happy, saying: "I felt we may have had a couple more in, but we are grateful for the recognition."

The full side was: Bryan King (Millwall), John Craggs (Boro), John Gorman (Carlisle), Bruce Rioch (Villa), Dave Watson (Sunderland), Willie Maddren (Boro), Duncan McKenzie (Forest),

Asa Hartford (West Brom), Don Masson (Notts County), Don Rogers (Palace), Dennis Tueart (Sunderland).

Willie Maddren all smiles after his nomination.

* * * * *

Double number four

CHARLTON made a promise to the fans ahead of Boro's game against Millwall.

"We're going to attack like hell," was the bold prediction.

"Seeing as they are a middle of the table side with no hope of promotion and no real fear of relegation, I am looking forward to them wanting to play."

The Lions had Gordon Bolland suspended. Frank Saul, a midfield stalwart formerly of Tottenham, Southampton and QPR, took his place.

Boro were at full strength.

* * * * *

SATURDAY MARCH 9
Middlesbrough 2   Millwall 1

MIDDLESBROUGH	MILLWALL
Platt	King
Craggs	Donaldson
Spraggon	Cripps
Souness	Dorney
Boam	Kitchener
Maddren	Allder
Murdoch	Saul
Mills	Clark
Hickton	Wood
Foggon	Smethurst
Armstrong	Hill
Sub: Smith	Sub: Brown

Scorers: Mills 8, Clark 10, Spraggon 79.

Attendance: 20,567.

Match Report

THE game was played on a very cold afternoon, with driving sleet making life awkward during the game and a torrential hailstorm just beforehand making life very sore off it.

Nevertheless it took Boro just eight minutes to find the back of the net, the third time in the last four matches they had scored in the opening ten minutes. Bobby Murdoch sent over a telling cross, Alan Foggon tapped it back and David Mills sent a crashing drive into the net.

The lead lasted just two minutes. Jim Platt made a fine save from Alf Wood, but could do nothing as Millwall kept up the pressure and after a frantic scramble inside Boro's box, Brian Clark turned in the equaliser from close range.

Millwall were soon back on the attack. Platt was twice called into action to keep the scores level. Another effort from Smethurst was well saved, while Wood flashed a header just wide.

Jack Charlton certainly had his wish granted that Millwall would want to come and play football! Boro re-grouped and began to cause problems. John Craggs shot over, David Mills had a header saved, while Bryan King, having been passed by Graeme Souness, swivelled to make a fantastic save.

Harry Cripps smashed the ball against his own bar when attempting a clearance and Alan Foggon wasted a glorious chance as Boro pressed. By now the home side were encamped in the Millwall half, King making two fine saves.

But he could do nothing about Boro's winner which came from Frank Spraggon, his first of the season. Boro's longest serving player scored what was only his third goal for the club since his debut ten years before when turning the ball in from close range following a mad scramble inside the box.

"The lads ran themselves into the ground in that second half. I was delighted with them and Millwall made a game of it," was the reaction of Charlton to the win.

"I want us to be competitive in every match, right through to the last one at Preston. People pay to come and watch us and they are entitled to the best."

– MAN OF THE MATCH –

MILLWALL'S manager Benny Fenton said very little when asked for his nomination for Boro's star man, in fact he said just one word: "CRAGGS."

Middlesbrough v Millwall
Saturday 9th March

Frank Spraggon's expression, centre, says it all, " I've just scored the winner against Millwall."

Second Division League Table - 8-3-74

	P	W	D	L	F	A	Pts
MIDDLESBROUGH	**31**	**19**	**10**	**2**	**46**	**22**	**48**
Luton Town	30	15	9	6	43	34	39
Orient	31	13	12	6	46	31	38
Blackpool	32	13	11	8	43	30	37
West Bromwich Albion	31	13	11	7	40	30	37
Nottingham Forest	31	11	13	7	43	39	35

– NEWS UPDATE –

Eventful week

THERE was an eventful week between Boro's home win over Millwall and their trip to The Hawthorns to take on West Brom.

Most of the squad had left immediately after the Millwall game and gone to Scarborough for a few days relaxation with the blessing of the club.

Golf, five-a-side on the beach and taking one of the many pleasant walks around Scarborough were all mixed in with light training sessions, with Charlton saying: "When they come back they will have a 100 per cent training session. It's punishment for all the luxuries they've probably indulged themselves in. But I'm sure they'll enjoy it!"

However, three Boro players were to be involved in an Under-23 international at St James' Park, Newcastle, between England and Scotland.

Willie Maddren had already been called up, while David Mills and Graeme Souness were late call-ups for England and Scotland respectively.

Kevin Beattie pulled out of the England squad, as did Trevor Francis and Kevin Keegan.

"It's great news," enthused Charlton. "David is a transformed player. The crowd used to get on to him, but now they are behind him. As for Graeme, I think he can get into the Scots' squad for the World Cup Finals in the summer."

Charlton revealed he had turned down the offer of a TV appearance in Manchester on the Friday, ahead of the Liverpool-Leeds game.

"I told the TV people that this was a tense time for us and I intended to be with my players at West Brom on Friday night."

Mills, Maddren and Souness all played in the Under-23 game, Mills opening the scoring after 17 minutes and having a goal disallowed for offside. Souness and Maddren both shaped up very well.

One of football's all-time greats moved into the Second Division when England's World Cup winning captain Bobby Moore left West Ham to join Fulham, who were due to entertain Boro in the near future.

There was a boost for Boro on the pitch when Carlisle were beaten at Aston Villa, which meant that Jack Charlton's boys needed just nine points from their final ten games to clinch promotion.

* * * * *

Bring on the Baggies

ASA Hartford said he would re-appear to face Boro after threatening to go on strike if he didn't get his game all the time!

Hartford said he would stay to try and help Albion win promotion, then leave.

Charlton warned his team: " This is one of the hardest games we will have played away all season."

* * * * *

SATURDAY MARCH 16

West Bromwich Albion 0   Middlesbrough 4

WEST BROMWICH ALBION	MIDDLESBROUGH
Latchford	Platt
Nisbet (Shaw 65)	Craggs
Wilson	Spraggon
Cantello	Souness
Wile	Boam
Robertson	Maddren
Johnston	Murdoch
Brown	Mills
Astle	Hickton
Hartford	Foggon
Glover	Armstrong
	Sub: Brine

Scorers: Foggon 32, Hickton 64, Souness 77, Hickton pen 80.

Attendance: 24,178.

Boro's Under-23 trio left to right, David Mills, Graeme Souness, and Willie Maddren.

Match Report

THIS was regarded by many as Boro's finest display of the season.

Playing their first game at The Hawthorns for 20 years, Boro played the first half facing a brilliant sun against a side which still harboured promotion hopes of its own.

The opening exchanges were tight, nothing was being given away and chances were limited. Indeed the first shot of the game from either side didn't come until the 17th minute.

Just over half an hour had passed when David Mills (later to join West Brom), burst through the middle. His cross was cleared but only to Bobby Murdoch, who found Alan Foggon and he hammered the ball past Peter Latchford to give Boro the lead.

Stuart Boam and Willie Maddren were soon in action to make headed clearances as Albion tried to hit back, although Boro were looking sharp on the break. Mills had a shot cleared off the the line by Asa Hartford, while Boam raced upfield to find Foggon, whose cross fell to Graeme Souness, who shot over the bar.

Boro began to take command shortly before half time and after the break continued their dominance.

Goal No. 2 came after 64 minutes. Boro had burst through on the left and John Hickton turned a fine shot beyond Latchford with an instinctive first time finish.

Mills had a shot blocked and then sent an overhead pass to Hickton, who had a header saved.

Mills then had one shot blocked and two saved before Boro went three up after 77 minutes.

Souness cut through the middle, drew the defence, played a one-two with Hickton and rounded off a fine move by sidefooting the ball past a bemused goalkeeper.

Three minutes later John Wile brought down Hickton inside the area and Big John himself scored from the spot.

"The game was never easy," said Charlton, adding: "But the way we set about winning it was tremendous. They were tight at the back, constructive in the middle and devastating up front.

"The passing of the team was excellent and the challenging great. Ian MacFarlane was sitting next to me and kept saying 'POETRY, SHEER POETRY'."

Fulham at Craven Cottage was the next stop. Their spy at The Hawthorns, Terry Medwin, left with the teasing of Charlton in his ears: "Now then Terry, has that given you the willies?"

Bad loser: Former England coach Don Howe watched his West Brom side mauled 4-0 by a rampant Middlesbrough team at the Hawthorns, and then refused to name a Man of the Match.

– MAN OF THE MATCH –

ALBION boss Don Howe refused to comment after the game and the decision was left to Harold Mayes. Mayes was the chief press officer for the 1966 World Cup and he couldn't split MILLS and SOUNESS. Mills for "non-stop harrassment, running and challenging", Souness for "high midfield skill".

Fantastic at Fulham

BORO now needed just six points to secure promotion after Forest beat Blackpool and Luton beat third placed Orient on Saturday. Luton were looking solid in second, but all eyes were now on Boro, who were in danger of running away with the division.

Fulham had signed Bobby Moore from West Ham the previous week, but he watched from the stands as his new club lost at Sunderland.

His debut was at Craven Cottage against the best side the Second Division had seen for a long, long time. Middlesbrough Football Club.

Fulham manager Alec Stock said before the game: "All the big names in football are going to be at the match. A whole host of managers, players and top brass have been on to us for tickets and we're flagged out of complimentaries.

"We had a glowing report of Boro on Saturday and this game should be a cracker. I hope Bobby Moore has a fairytale debut. Moore has everything Fulham needs at the moment and I want to see his skill and knowledge rub off on our younger players."

Moore had a nightmare.

*   *   *   *   *

TUESDAY MARCH 19

Fulham 0   Middlesbrough 4

FULHAM	**MIDDLESBROUGH**
Mellor	Platt
Cutbush	Craggs
Slough (Strong 29)	Spraggon
Moore	Souness
Lacey	Boam
Dunne	Maddren
Conway	Murdoch (Smith 74)
Mullery	Mills
Busby	Hickton
Lloyd	Foggon
Barrett	Armstrong

Scorers: Maddren 32, Souness 75, Maddren 82, Boam 87.

Attendance: 18,114.

- MAN OF THE MATCH -

FULHAM boss Alec Stock couldn't split GRAEME SOUNESS and ALAN FOGGON, explaining: "Souness was outstanding in midfield and Foggon never let up in his chasing from start to finish."

Match Report

BORO opened up an 11 point gap at the top and needed just another four points for promotion, with eight matches left, after winning this in impressive style.

"We have convinced the people of the Midlands and London that we are a great team," said Charlton afterwards, adding: "We now have to convince the people of Middlesbrough. If we don't fill Ayresome Park next week we will never fill it."

Platitudes and praise were flowing in equal measure after Boro turned on the style in the Capital. One up after 32 minutes, Boro never looked back.

The opener, a header by Willie Maddren from a David Armstrong free kick, ensured that every outfield regular player had scored that season. Maddren added a second eight minutes from time, heading in an Armstrong corner.

In between Souness had hammered in from 20 yards with just a quarter of an hour remaining, while Stuart Boam, not letting Maddren away with scoring, added Boro's fourth a minute from time.

Boro, who covered the ground at great speed, gave Fulham a lesson. After a relatively quiet opening 45 minutes in which Fulham lost left-back Slough with a facial injury and Boro scored, Charlton's men turned on the style in the second half.

"It was our biggest defeat of the season, but we have no complaints," admitted Fulham manager Alec Stock.

"Boro have obviously learned a lot since we beat them up there at the start of the season."

Comedian Jimmy Tarbuck (below), was an interested spectator, saying: " All I can say is this Middlesbrough team are magic. They are as good as the Liverpool team which won promotion from the Second Division and I can't give any side higher praise than that."

Football mad entertainer Jimmy Tarbuck, after watching the Boro's five star performance against Fulham, compared their potential to Bill Shankly's great Liverpool side of the 1960s.

England's 1966 World Cup winning captain Bobby Moore (white shirt), here pictured with left to right, Harold Shepherdson, Nobby Stiles, Pat Partridge and Sir Alf Ramsey before Shep's testimonial match in May 1973, chose the wrong night to make his Fulham debut as Boro destroyed his new club 4-0 at Craven Cottage.

– NEWS UPDATE –

McAndrew honoured again

SHORTLY after the game at Fulham, Tony McAndrew received a call into the Scotland Under-17 squad to play Belgium in the second leg of a European Youth championship qualifying tie at Somerset Park, Ayr.

"I'm pleased to be in the squad," enthused McAndrew. "I played in our 2-1 win over there, but I thought I had been dropped because I hadn't heard anything after that game.

"It would be great to play in this one. We need only a point to qualify for the finals in Sweden in May."

McAndrew's hopes were dashed just 24 hours later when, playing for Boro's reserves at York, he went up for a high ball, landed awkwardly and broke his arm.

*   *   *   *   *

Up the Boro

BORO, who had won promotion from the Third Division when beating Oxford in 1967, hoped that a repeat performance was on the cards.

If any two of Orient, Forest and Carlisle were to lose, Boro would be promoted provided they themselves won.

The fans were almost implored by Charlton to get to the game. He said: "My players have earned decent crowds by their displays this season and it will be a shame if anyone misses out on the celebrations which may take place.

"There is no champagne on ice, but I'm sure it wouldn't take long to rustle some up!

"Oxford are desperate for points and will make things hard for us."

Oxford were unbeaten in their previous four games and Boro's build up had been interrupted by injuries to John Craggs (three stitches in a leg gash), Bobby Murdoch and Alan Foggon, both of whom had thigh strains.

*   *   *   *   *

SATURDAY MARCH 23

Middlesbrough 1   Oxford United 0

MIDDLESBROUGH	OXFORD UNITED
Platt	Burton
Craggs	Light
Spraggon	Shuker
Souness	Roberts
Boam	Clarke
Maddren	Briggs
Murdoch	Gough (Skeen 80)
Mills	Atkinson
Hickton	Curran
Foggon	Clarke
Armstrong	Aylott
Sub: Brine	

Scorer: Armstrong 72.

Attendance: 26,877.

Match Report

OXFORD made it as hard as possible for Boro, who had to rely on a single goal to make promotion a mathematical certainty.

There was a degree of nervousness about their display, understandably, but nerves were calmed when David Armstrong turned in his fifth goal of the season after 72 minutes, sparking celebrations all around the ground.

No-one cared less about the standard of the game that afternoon. All the Boro fans were concerned about was their result and the results from the other three matches.

The news filtered through that Orient had lost, but Carlisle had drawn.......followed by an anxious wait for the next result. But the wait was worthwhile as it was confirmed that Forest had lost and Boro were back in the First Division for the first time in 20 years, achieving promotion with seven games still to be played.

"I have never won anything before," beamed Willie Maddren. "I didn't even get a Durham County trial as a schoolboy."

Chairman Charles Amer scampered away to his car, returning with a case of champagne which he had kept in his boot and refused to bring into the ground until the news was confirmed.

Amer's reaction to promotion? "It has been a team effort from the boardroom to the dressing room. Everybody who has worked for Middlesbrough Football Club has been treated right. I have been ruthlessly fair. That goes for the staff, the team and the fans."

Charlton didn't want to say too much, preferring the praise to be heaped elsewhere: "Write about the players," he said. "I get embarrassed at times when people write and talk about what I have done.

"This team will be going into the First Division to compete. I do not believe in trying to survive. The players have got a taste for success and believe me they will want more.

"But we still have unfinished business in this division. We can win the championship next week at Luton and I can now start looking around at other matches and at players who I want to strengthen my team."

– MAN OF THE MATCH –

THE Oxford manager Gerry Summers nominated GRAEME SOUNESS, then revealed that he had almost bought the player before he signed for Boro.

"The Spurs manager Bill Nicholson came on the phone to me over a year ago and said he was keeping his word, that Souness, who we had enquired about before, was now available for sale.

"He told me that there was one other club in opposition and that the price was £30,000. We couldn't pay that kind of money, so he went to Boro."

Souness, meanwhile, was still in the Boro dressing room when he was told he had been called into the full Scotland squad to play West Germany in Frankfurt the following Wednesday.

The goal that secured promotion. David Armstrong scores against Oxford in the Bob End at Ayresome Park.

Cheers everybody: Division One here we come !

REFLECTIONS

John Hickton

BIG JOHN had been leading scorer with Boro every season bar one - his first, when John O'Rourke was the leading hit man - since he joined as a defender from Sheffield Wednesday.

Hickton had left the Hillsborough club in September, 1966. Things hadn't been the same since he was left out of the team which lost the FA Cup Final to Everton.

The Owls manager, Alan Brown, was a friend of then Boro manager Stan Anderson and as result of that association came Hickton's transfer to Middlesbrough, which took place for a fee of £20,000.

Playing as a centre-half and a right-back, with only occasional games up front, Hickton scored 15 goals in his first season, 24 in his second and it was not until his third season that he was moved to a permanent position up front.

Ironically, in 1973-74, the most successful of all seasons he enjoyed with the club, Hickton scored fewer goals than he had done in any preceding season.

"I never thought I would see the day when I said that it didn't matter who scored the goals," confesses the big man. "But that season things were going so well, it didn't really matter who put them in, as long as someone did.

"Beforehand, if we won 5-0 and I hadn't scored, I wasn't happy. I hadn't done my job. But I had a slightly different role under Jack and it was Alan Foggon who did most of the scoring."

The change of heart from Hickton was brought about by one thing.

"Team spirit," said John. "We had a tremendous team spirit then. I'd never known anything like it. Everyone was pulling for everyone else and you just didn't want to be the one who let anyone down.

"I'd been around a bit, but I hadn't seen anything like that before. Normally you would find one or two in the dressing room who would play but didn't mix in, but not this team. It was as if we were one family."

Hickton went on: "Everyone was excited when Jack came. He had done everything in the game and it was him who brought everyone together, not that there was a major problem before.

"The feeling in the dressing room which we had then must have been like the one the present day lads had when Bryan Robson arrived. He had done almost everything in the game and that demands respect."

The mixture worked. All of a sudden teams which had caused problems before were turned over, dominated in a way not always reflected in the scoreline.

Teams like Oxford, Sunderland and Swindon, not forgetting Sheffield Wednesday.

"I got a lot of satisfaction about whacking them at the end of that season," says Hickton, sporting a huge grin.

"Eight-nil and I scored early. I must have softened them up for the other lads.

"We didn't struggle against many sides. We had our off days, it wasn't all plain sailing, but there were not many sides who we didn't get the better of."

In fact Boro failed to beat only four sides, home or away, all season, drawing twice against Villa, Orient and Blackpool, and drawing and losing to Bolton. However when Boro played them, twice in less than a week, the Trotters had just signed England international winger Peter Thompson from Liverpool.

Collectively, teams didn't pose too much of a threat to Boro that year. Individually there didn't appear anyone who the lads were apprehensive of playing against.

"I was never frightened of playing against anyone," says Hickton unsurprisingly. "When you were playing right down the middle you often came across big centre-halves like Barry Kitchener at Millwall, but in those days you always found that you earned the respect of your opponent if you gave as good as you got. In that role it was also up to you to intimidate the goalkeeper!"

Most fans remember Hickton the penalty taker, a fearsome sight for those behind the goal, as well as those between the sticks, in case the net burst with the power of delivery.

"Believe it or not I used to sidefoot my kicks. Even today people come up and say I remember you starting your run up at the half-way line! Well that wasn't quite the case. I would go to the edge of the penalty box sometimes, most times. But I always used to try and place the kicks sidefooted. I still managed some power in them though!"

Did anyone ever try to take a kick ahead of John?

"David Armstrong tried to take one instead of me once, when he was just a young lad. He didn't try too often again!"

Like most of the players, Hickton picks two matches which seemed to sum up the season as a whole.

"West Brom and Fulham," he says, without hesitation.

"I think it was generally recognised that our display in winning 4-0 at West Brom was probably our best of the season.

"We followed that up when winning three days later at Craven Cottage, same score. Our next game saw us win promotion, the one after that we won the league. There was no stopping us.

"The same system worked for us in the First Division for a while, but seasons like '73-'74 only come once in a lifetime."

CHAPTER ELEVEN

APRIL

– NEWS UPDATE –

Testimonial

BORO were back in training on the Monday following their win over Oxford and were back in action on the pitch the following night after keeping an agreement to play in a testimonial game for Alan Sproates at Darlington.

Boro went 3-0 up in the opening 12 minutes and were then reminded that it was only a testimonial! They eased down, eventually winning 4-0.

A decent crowd of 5,000 turned up and watched Foggon, 2, Mills and Boam score the goals, while Sproates missed a giveaway penalty in his own game!

Earlier, in the warm up game, Jack Charlton had scored two goals for Darlington against a Darlington All Stars XI.

*   *   *   *   *

Simply champion

BORO'S recently formed supporters club had hired the League Liner for the game against Luton at Kenilworth Road a few weeks earlier at the beginning of the month.

Little did they know at the time that they would be attending a promotion party which could see their side crowned as champions.

The League Liner was a luxury 500 seater passenger train which originally had a 42 seat cinema and a disco on board, but British Rail, who hired the train to clubs, had withdrawn those facilities as they were too expensive.

Boro's supporters were the first to hire the train without having any alcohol on board, prompting league spokesman Albert Howcroft to say: "They must all be Methodists up there!"

The fare was £3 for adults and £2 for juveniles, which compared favourably with the air fare, which was £22 a head.

A win for Boro would give them the title, while a win for Luton would almost guarantee the Hatters promotion.

"Sometimes these matches have a habit of dying," said Luton manager Harry Haslam. "But I don't think this one will. This game can show the world of football the wonderfully high level the game has reached in the Second Division.

"Everyone said three-up and three-down would lead to defensive play, but I haven't seen that at all. As for Boro, they are a tremendously improved side. Their small players are 6' 2", the big blokes 7' 6". It's a good job Jack Charlton can't grow any taller. I wouldn't be able to speak with him."

Haslam had sent Boro a telegram saying: "Good luck on promotion. Keep that First Division bed warm for us."

Meanwhile a team of steel erectors working in the South had painted the words 'Boro 4 Luton 0' on metal girders at a local ironworks.

*   *   *   *   *

SATURDAY MARCH 30
Luton Town 0   Middlesbrough 1

LUTON TOWN	MIDDLESBROUGH
Horn	Platt
John Ryan	Craggs
Thomson	Cochrane
Anderson	Souness
Faulkner	Boam
Garner	Maddren
Jimmy Ryan	Murdoch
Husband	Mills
Butlin	Hickton
West	Foggon
Aston	Armstrong
Sub: Hindson	Sub: Smith

Scorer: Mills 76.

Attendance: 19,812.

David Mills scored the goal which won the championship for Middlesbrough at Kenilworth Road.

Match Report

FRANK Spraggon had been confined to bed on the Thursday prior to the game suffering with 'flu. His place was taken by Jimmy Cochrane, who had last played in early December when making his debut against Sheffield Wednesday.

Thousands of Boro fans had made the journey, taking up almost three sides of the ground, but they had to wait a while before they had the championship to celebrate.

The team lined up inside the centre circle to wave to the fans before kick-off before starting the game in determined mood. While the previous week's promotion winning match was nothing to write home about, this was a keenly fought and entertaining affair, if not one of the highest standard.

Two Boro players, Murdoch and Cochrane, were booked in the opening half hour, while both sides went close to scoring in a wide open game.

Jim Platt saved a low Barry Butlin header comfortably, while Stuart Boam headed just over the bar at the other end.

A drive from John Craggs was blocked, while Platt was forced to concede a corner when the ball bounced awkwardly in front of him from an Alan Garner throw.

Graeme Souness had a strong shot deflected wide, while John Aston had a strong shot blocked.

A high backpass from Boam had Platt at full stretch, but then Boro broke to take the lead. Murdoch found Alan Foggon, away on Boro's right wing. His cross found Mills, who brought the ball under control, swivelled and hit a fine shot in off the far post.

Boro had some serious defending to do to prevent conceding an equaliser and Alan West was unlucky with a deflected shot.

But they were Boro's points and with it came the Second Division Championship with six matches still to play.

> ## – MAN OF THE MATCH –
> WILLIE MADDREN was the choice of Harry Haslam: *"He was a master in the air and was always right in the thick of things. He had an excellent match."*

Just Champion: The celebrations begin after a 1-0 victory over Luton at Kenilworth Road secured Middlesbrough the Second Division Championship.

– NEWS UPDATE –

Captain's comments

CAPTAIN Stuart Boam (right), summed up the feelings of the team and probably the town as he said: "If somebody had said at the beginning of the season we would be the champions with six games still to be played I would have laughed at them.

"We've been lucky with injuries. It has been much the same team week after week and the more you play with each other, the better the understanding.

"We expected to beat Luton, but that was borne out of confidence, not complacency. The lads' character has been shown by the way they have stuck to Jack Charlton's methods of play from start to finish.

"As captain, I couldn't have asked for a better set of lads. Even off the park, if I have asked them to do something they have gone out of their way to help. If we can keep the same lads together, I can't see many teams beating us, even the cream of the First Division."

Stuart Boam. Proud Captain.

* * * * *

Mauling of the Magpies

GRAEME Souness was confined to bed with a temperature of 101 the following week. The same virus had laid low Frank Spraggon and also affected Bill Gates and Peter Brine.

Brine had recovered in time for the game against Notts County and took the place of Souness.

It was Boro's first match since being crowned champions and the first match back at Ayresome for Don Masson, who had been transferred to County for £5,000 in 1968.

"There can be no let up," insisted Charlton. "We still have a lot to learn and a lot of work to do."

Charlton was named Manager Of The Month for March and would receive a gallon of Bell's Scotch Whisky and a cheque for £100.

"I have to thank the lads for the way they performed in what I thought was going to be a really difficult month. Two at home and four away have brought six wins, 12 points, promotion and the championship. It is a tremendous achievement by the lads and I am only as good as them."

* * * * *

Custodian praises the defence

Goalkeeper Jim Platt (right) was full of praise for his team, saying: "The lads in front of me have been absolutely brilliant. If I had my pick of the country as a whole, I would not choose anyone else but our present back-four.

"This has been a fantastic season, easily the best of my career and I'm sure our success has not ended. With players like these in Boro's side we should really do well in the First Division."

Including cup games, Platt had kept 24 clean sheets up to and including the Luton match.

Jim Platt: King of the clean sheets.

* * * * *

SATURDAY APRIL 6
Middlesbrough 4   Notts County 0

MIDDLESBROUGH	NOTTS COUNTY
Platt	McManus
Craggs	Brindley
Spraggon	O'Brien
Brine (McMordie 82)	Bolton (Nixon 58)
Boam	Needham
Maddren	Stubbs
Murdoch	Randall
Smith	Masson
Hickton	Bradd
Foggon	McVey
Armstrong	Mann

Scorers: Hickton 47, Needham o.g. 53, Armstrong 70, Foggon 72.

Attendance: 27,823.

Match Report

DAVID Mills reported ill on the morning of the game with a temperature very similar to that suffered by Souness. He was immediately sent home and Malcolm Smith was called up to start a game for the first time for five months. Peter Brine was starting a game for the first time in six weeks.

Eric McMordie, although substitute, was to play a part for the first time since the middle of November. It was to be the last of 266 appearances in a Boro shirt in a career which started when playing in a 2-2 draw at Plymouth in 1965. McMordie was to go later to Sheffield Wednesday and York before retiring from the game.

Boro's players kicked 24 plastic footballs into the crowd and handed out six bouquets of flowers to lady supporters before the kick-off.

Luton consolidated their second placing with a 4-2 home win over Preston, while Orient edged back into third with a 1-1 home draw over Millwall. Carlisle lost 2-0 at Bristol City.

Boro, meanwhile, recorded their biggest home win of the season to date. After a goalless first half, during which Alan Foggon saw an overhead kick cleared off the line by left-half Brian Stubbs, Boro moved into overdrive in the second 45 minutes.

The opening goal came two minutes into the restart. David Armstrong cut through to bring a save out of Eric McManus and the rebound fell to John Hickton, whose shot was blocked by centre-half Dave Needham. But there was no mistake from the second rebound, Hickton hammering into the net.

Six minutes later Smith raced though and sent over a good cross which was intended for Alan Foggon, but Needham, attempting a clearance, slammed the ball into his own net.

Armstrong then almost burst the net with the first of two goals in as many minutes.

On 70 minutes a Smith cross was pulled back by Hickton into the path of the 19 year old Durham lad who smashed home with some power, while two minutes later a crashing drive from Foggon asserted Boro's superiority.

Despite the constant probing and urging of Masson, Boro were, quite simply, a class apart.

"I'm delighted we have given an 'away' performance at home," said Stuart Boam.

"The margin of the victory may have been greater, but it was a good day and the fans were great."

– MAN OF THE MATCH –

COUNTY boss Jimmy Sirrell nominated both HICKTON and BOAM.
"I was tempted to make it Hickton," he said, adding: "But we were on top for a little while in the first half and Boam held the defence together."

John Hickton begins the 4-0 second half demolition of Notts County by threading the opening goal through a posse of Magpie defenders.

– NEWS UPDATE –

Debut

AFTER six years understudying Willie Whigham and Jim Platt, Pat Cuff made his debut between the posts in a Middlesbrough shirt.

Graeme Souness and David Mills had recovered from their viral infections and were included in the side, but Frank Spraggon was rested as Jimmy Cochrane played another match.

* * * * *

Young 'keeper Pat Cuff celebrated his debut against Bolton by confidently keeping a clean sheet.

TUESDAY APRIL 9
Middlesbrough 0   Bolton Wanderers 0

MIDDLESBROUGH	BOLTON WANDERERS
Cuff	Siddall
Craggs	Ritson
Cochrane	Nicholson
Souness	McAllister
Boam	P.Jones
Maddren	Waldron
Murdoch	Olinyk
Mills	G.Jones
Hickton	Greaves
Foggon (Brine 79)	Whatmore
Armstrong	Thompson
	Sub: Lee

Attendance: 28,143.

Match Report

Cochrane enjoyed a fine game, while Cuff kept a clean sheet in an encouraging first appearance, making a brilliant save to deny Gary Jones in the first half. John Craggs had his work cut out to keep former Liverpool winger Peter Thompson quiet when the visitors decided to attack.

But the game, Boro's penultimate home fixture, was a huge let down in front of the second largest crowd of the season. Only the attendance against Sunderand on Boxing Day was larger.

Bolton went to Ayresome to defend. Boro, described later as "too aristocratic" in their approach, woke up a shade in the second half under splendid prompting from Graeme Souness, but the closest they came to scoring was when they had two penalty appeals turned down.

Right-back John Ritson appeared to handle the ball, while David Mills was bundled over inside the box. But neither decision went in favour of a Boro side whose manager offered the following assessment of a dull sort of game.

Charlton said: "The game was too tight for this time of the season. Both teams should have played it more openly to give the crowd more entertainment and a goal or two. My lads tried hard enough. It was very frustrating for them."

– MAN OF THE MATCH –

THE gentlemen of the press box gave a unanimous vote to GRAEME SOUNESS, with the general feeling summed up with a statement which read:
"His obvious class made him stand out. There is one player the First Division won't worry."

– NEWS UPDATE –

No Easter gifts for Boro

BORO went into the Easter programme knowing they were just two points away from equalling a post-war Second Division points record, jointly held by Leeds and Derby.

The long haul to South Wales was made on Easter Saturday. Jim Platt returned in goal and Frank Spraggon at left-back, while Peter Brine was favoured ahead of Bobby Murdoch and Malcolm Smith ahead of John Hickton as Charlton kept his promise of "changing a few things around towards the end of the season".

The Cardiff manager Frank O'Farrell was due to take over as manager of the Iranian national team and left team affairs at Ninian Park in the hands of his assistant Jimmy Andrews. His side were fighting for their Second Division lives.

* * * * *

SATURDAY APRIL 13
Cardiff City 3   Middlesbrough 2

CARDIFF CITY	MIDDLESBROUGH
Healey	Platt
Dwyer	Craggs
Pethard	Spraggon
Charles	Souness
Morgan	Boam
Villars	Maddren
Reece	Brine (Murdoch 61)
Vincent	Mills
Phillips	Smith
Carlin	Foggon
Anderson	Armstrong
Sub: Showers	

Scorers: Reece 6, Carlin 38, Maddren 58,
           Vincent 64, Foggon 88.

Attendance: 12,856.

Former Boro midfielder, Johnny Vincent, scored for Cardiff as the Welsh side inflicted only the third league defeat of the season on the Boro, with a 3-2 win at Ninian Park.

Match Report

WHATEVER the reason - and none was offered - Boro well and truly had an off day as they suffered what was just their third defeat of the season.

The tone of the day was set as early as the sixth minute when Boro conceded a soft goal.

Alan Foggon had gone close in the opening minute, but that proved to be rare chance as the Welshmen took control.

With just six minutes gone Stuart Boam looked to have been guilty of obstruction. Jim Platt thought he had heard the whistle and stood on his line watching as Tony Villars crossed to Gil Reece who headed into the net!

Control was difficult on a bright but cold and blustery day, but Cardiff were certainly up for the game and thought they had won a penalty when the ball hit Frank Spraggon's hand inside the box. Nothing was given, but City soon went two-up.

Spraggon conceded a free-kick after 38 minutes. A deep ball was headed back from the far post by Phil Dwyer to Willie Carlin, who stooped low to head past Platt.

Reece, unmarked ten yards out, should have made it three, but hesitated when he should have shot. Platt tipped a Villars piledriver on to the bar, the rebound caused a melee in Boro's box and Spraggon had to clear off the line.

Boro surprisingly pulled one back after 58 minutes when Willie Maddren powerfully headed a David Armstrong cross beyond the reach of Ron Healey.

It took just six minutes for the Bluebirds to return to a two goal advantage.

Two players were to score against their former clubs as the match continued.

Alan Foggon had been transferred from Cardiff for £10,000 the previous season, while Johnny Vincent left Ayresome in 1972 after making 39 appearances for the club after joining from Birmingham City in a swop deal which saw George Smith go to St Andrews a year earlier.

Vincent took great delight in rattling one past Boro after 64 minutes. A long ball from Fred Pethard fell to Vincent, who easily bypassed the outcoming Platt to shoot into an empty net.

Boro rallied and applied pressure for the first time in the game. Armstrong had a header cleared off the line, but there was no stopping Foggon, who hammered in with just two minutes to go.

The result was almost certain to keep Cardiff in the division.

– MAN OF THE MATCH –

A consortium of Welsh pressmen gave the nod to WILLIE MADDREN, saying: "His defensive contribution was excellent and his headed goal gave him the edge over Souness and Boam."

– NEWS UPDATE –

Double trouble

JACK Charlton, Harold Shepherdson, together with coaches Ian MacFarlane and Jimmy Greenhalgh, were watching prospective transfer targets and therefore missed the game which saw Boro's second defeat in three days following the magnificent run of only two defeats in more than seven months.

* * * * *

MONDAY APRIL 15

Bolton Wanderers 2   Middlesbrough 1

BOLTON WANDERERS	MIDDLESBROUGH
Siddall	Cuff
Ritson	Creamer
Nicholson	Spraggon
McAllister	Souness
Allardyce	Boam
Waldron	Maddren
Olinyk	Murdoch
G Jones	Mills
Byron	Hickton (Brine 46)
Whatmore	Foggon
Thompson	Armstrong
Sub: Darling	

Scorers: Byrom 18, G.Jones 51, Boam 86.

Attendance: 22,545.

Match Report

Boro made four changes from the side which lost at Cardiff, the most they made for any one match all season.

Pat Cuff returned in goal, Peter Creamer came in for John Craggs, while Bobby Murdoch came in for Peter Brine, who was relegated to a substitute's role. John Hickton returned up front ahead of Malcolm Smith, who had broken his nose in South Wales.

However, Boro were again well and truly beaten by a better organised, more determined side, although they should have gone into lead after 15 minutes when Alan Foggon missed an open goal.

Three minutes later Byrom was allowed to waltz through a hesitant defence and slam one in off the post.

Garry Jones headed a second after 51 minutes, while Boro reduced the arrears when Stuart Boam, up supporting the attack as he often liked to do, headed a consolation goal four minutes from time.

Graeme Souness picked up a booking which meant he would miss the final game of the season at Preston, while Boro were left with a few injuries after the weekend's matches as Creamer, who had sustained knee ligament damage, Spraggon a slightly less serious knee injury and John Hickton a kick on the calf, joined Smith on the injured list.

> ## – MAN OF THE MATCH –
>
> *JIMMY Armfield, who was in charge at Bolton at the time, selected WILLIE MADDREN and DAVID ARMSTRONG as joint recipients for "their tireless work".*

Bolton Wanderers, managed by former England full-back Jimmy Armfield (right), condemned the Boro to their second defeat in three days with a 2-1 win at Burnden Park.

New Faces

JACK Charlton spoke for the first time about bringing new faces in for the season ahead prior to Boro's final home game of the season.

A total of seven matches had been covered by he and his coaching staff over the Easter programme, with Charlton saying: "It's not the best time of year to be looking at players, but it's the first real chance I've had. I didn't see a lot, apart from the £300,000-£350,000 players who I knew about anyway.

"The trouble is that some of the better players have lost their edge and because they aren't doing so much, some of the less talented players are able to show up better. But I do need some new men. If I get hit by injuries next season it would be worrying."

* * * * *

Season ticket prices

IT was announced that season ticket prices would rise for the following season.

The best seats would rise from £14 to £25 for the season, still half the rate of the most expensive clubs in the top flight.

Chairman Charles Amer explained the need for a rise, saying: "We have made a survey throughout the four divisions and have come to a realistic price which we feel will enable us to go a long way towards meeting the increased costs of running a First Division football club.

"We have a great deal of work to do on the ground to keep pace with the image of having a team from this area in the First Division. While we are very proud of what we have already, we still have got to keep going ahead."

The prices for the 1974-75 season would be: Centre Stand £25, Wing Stand £20, North Terrace and East End £18, South Terrace £12. Standing on the Holgate End and in front of the East End seats was to be 50p per match.

These prices compared favourably with current season prices with other clubs for the best seats, such as Arsenal £49.50, Newcastle £25 and Sunderland £19, bearing in mind those prices would rise in the summer and Sunderland fans were watching Second Division football.

"We are looking forward to seeing our team play against all the best sides in the country and with our improved facilities we are going to show nothing is too good for Boro fans," enthused Amer.

It was revealed that Boro were to spend £140,000-£150,000 on improvements at Ayresome Park, increasing the capacity from 40,000 to somewhere between 43-44,000.

The first nine rows of the East End seats were to be taken out and turned into a boys enclosure and a standing area for season-ticket holders. The changes would see 1,000 seats taken out, with the capacity for 3,000 standing in its place. The current boys enclosure would be turned over for adults.

Larger, brick built, food and soft drink bars and a new siting for TV cameras on top of the South Stand were to be added, together with a complete new roof for the South Stand, as well as alterations to certain seating and sections of terracing.

A new floodlighting system was to be installed, four times stronger than the original one, to accommodate the needs of the cameras for colour TV.

* * * * *

Transfer news

FOUR players were to receive free transfers at the end of the season, Malcolm Poskett, Bobby Huntingdon, Maurice Gormley and Frank McGivern, while Bill Gates was to retire after his testimonial to concentrate on his sports shop business.

* * * * *

Owls obliterated as Boro equal record

RELEGATION threatened Sheffield Wednesday had injury worries, but Boro had rid themselves of all theirs as they prepared for their final home game of the season.

Boro needed just two points to equal the Second Division post-war points record and were determined to give their fans a send-off in style.

The Football League president Len Shipman presented Boro with the Second Division trophy and winners' medals before the kick-off. The trophy was received by Charles Amer, the medals by the players.

"The lads want to finish the season on a high note and they'll be trying all the way to get a good result," said Charlton, adding: "If we're going to help our kid (at relegation threatened Preston) that's the way we'll do it and he'll have to take his chance next Saturday."

* * * * *

SATURDAY APRIL 20

Middlesbrough 8	Sheffield Wednesday 0

MIDDLESBROUGH	**SHEFFIELD WEDNESDAY**
Platt	Springett
Craggs	Rodrigues
Spraggon	Shaw
Souness	Mullen
BoamHolsgrove	
Maddren	Coyle (Eustace 46)
Murdoch (Charlton 60)	Potts
Mills	Prudham
Hickton	Joicey
Foggon	Craig
Armstrong	Cameron

Scorers: Hickton 5, Mills 14, Murdoch 35, Souness 53, Souness 70, Foggon 72, Souness 79, Foggon 87.

Attendance: 25,287.

Hat-trick hero Graeme Souness relaxes in style after his outstanding performance against Sheffield Wednesday. Nice flares Graeme!

105

Match Report

IT took Boro just five minutes to start building what turned out to be their biggest win for 16 years, a win which failed by one goal to equal the all time club record.

Boro had beaten Brighton 9-0 in the opening game of the 1958-59 season, but had come nowhere near it since.

Graeme Souness set the move going, and Alan Foggon evaded his markers and crossed into the penalty area where John Hickton rose high to head in.

Foggon was again involved in the build-up as Boro doubled their advantage after 14 minutes.

His through ball found David Mills, whose cool finish saw him lob over the top of the advancing goalkeeper.

No. 3 arrived ten minutes before the break. A long ball out of defence was collected by Hickton. He stormed through and crossed to the back post, where Foggon received and immediately laid off to Bobby Murdoch, who slammed past the helpless Springett.

Apart from the three goals, Boro had created a bagful of chances in the opening 45 minutes and left the field to a standing ovation.

It didn't take long for the rout to continue - eight minutes to be precise. John Craggs whipped a ball out to Hickton, and his cross fell to Souness, who trapped the ball, looked up, picked his spot and slid it into the far corner.

Shock! Wednesday broke, Brian Joicey's shot beat Jim Platt and Stuart Boam had to clear off the line.

Harry Charlton replaced Murdoch after an hour, the Scot going off to tremendous applause.

Boro's fifth came ten minutes later, as Wednesday cleared a corner, but only to Souness, who smashed in his second of the game. Two minutes later Foggon added a sixth when racing in unchecked from the left to smash a powerful drive goalbound. Springett claimed the ball hadn't crossed the line, but the referee was having none of it, feeling, as did the crowd, that the sheer power of the shot had carried it over.

Souness completed what was to be his one and only hat trick for the club, scoring his third 26 minutes after his first, having been picked out unselfishly by David Mills.

Wednesday had a goal disallowed after the ball was punched in, but Boro were not finished scoring, adding their eighth, with Foggon's second, three minutes from time.

Wednesday manager Steve Burtenshaw said: "Boro gave one of the best all-round displays I have seen for years. But my lads deserve to have their backsides kicked for a shoddy display. Boro are a very good team, but they're not eight goals better than Wednesday."

Charlton's reaction said it all: "The lads did us proud and showed the sort of spirit we want them to show. The one thing they must learn is to be ruthless and they went a long way towards that today. I felt a bit sorry for Wednesday."

Results elsewhere almost certainly meant that Preston would go down when they met Boro in the final match of the season.

To survive, Bobby Charlton's side would have to beat Boro 5-0 and hope Wednesday lost 3-0 at home to Bolton.

"I'm disappointed that Preston look certain to go down," said Jack. "For our kid's sake."

– MAN OF THE MATCH –

STEVE Burtenshaw nominated GRAEME SOUNESS, saying simply: "He hardly wasted a ball in 90 minutes......then there was his hat-trick!"

Thanks for your support: The Boro players proudly parade their championship trophy for the fans following the 8-0 thrashing of Sheffield Wednesday.

No let up in Norway

BORO flew to Norway for a friendly game on the Tuesday before the final match of the season.

They beat Brann in Bergen 4-0 with goals coming from Alan Foggon (right) after 17 seconds and 17 minutes, Bobby Murdoch on 55 minutes and Willie Maddren five minutes from time.

A crowd of 9,200 turned up to watch the game.

Alan Foggon:
Norse double.

Meanwhile Leeds United were crowned First Division Champions for the second time in five years on the Wednesday, as Arsenal beat Liverpool to end the title challenge of the Merseysiders.

* * * * *

Preston polished off by record breakers

A draw in the final game of the season would give Boro an all time points record for the Second Division. Their win over Wednesday had already seen them equal a record 63 points, jointly held by Leeds and Derby.

Peter Brine replaced the suspended Graeme Souness against a Preston side which had won only one of its previous 12 matches and one which had Nobby Stiles missing, like Souness, through suspension.

Peter Brine proved himself to be an ideal replacement for
Graeme Souness when he scored twice in the Boro's final league
game of the season, a 4-2 victory over Preston at Deepdale.

"It's a pity this game isn't going to be the relegation type battle it looked like being at one stage," said Jack beforehand.

"Preston would have to beat us by a sackful and I'm afraid that's just not on. It would be a coward's way out to say I hoped it would be settled one way or the other before we went there. I'd have liked to see them still have something to fight for and we would not have made it easy for them by any means.

"It would have been better if they had been clear altogether of course. It must be terribly disappointing for Bobby."

The Football Association had docked Preston one point in December for playing an ineligible player. Dave Carrick, who was substitute at Oxford on November 17, had been signed during the week leading up to that game from Cheshire League club Witton Albion.

His registration had not come through in time and the club were fined £200, as well as having the point docked, but it made no difference to their league position at the end of the season.

Boro's fans again travelled by the League Liner.

* * * * *

SATURDAY APRIL 27

Preston North End 2   Middlesbrough 4

PRESTON NORTH END	MIDDLESBROUGH
Brown	Platt
McMahon	Craggs
Spark	Spraggon
Baxter	Brine
Hawkins	Boam
Bird	Maddren
Morley	Murdoch
Burns	Mills
Elwiss	Hickton
Treacy	Foggon
Sadler	Armstrong
Sub: Lamb	Sub: Charlton

Scorers: Brine 6, Foggon 19, Hickton 25, Elwiss 29, Elwiss 43, Foggon 51.

Attendance: 16,177.

- MAN OF THE MATCH -

BOBBY Charlton gave the final vote of the season to
JIM PLATT, without giving a reason.

Match Report

BORO went three up in the opening 25 minutes to all but secure what would be their ninth double of the season.

Just six minutes had elapsed when a drive from Alan Foggon was too strong for goalkeeper John Brown to hold. The ball could have gone anywhere but fell to Peter Brine, who ran in to head home.

Ray Treacy flashed a shot just wide as Preston tried to hit back, but it was Boro who scored again after 19 minutes. A David Armstrong corner was headed on by Stuart Boam, and Brine headed it in turn to Foggon, who completed the heading movement by nodding into the net.

Boro were three-up on 25 minutes. John Craggs burst through on the right and crossed to John Hickton, who rose high at the back post to thunder a header past Brown.

Preston pulled one back just four minutes later. A Francis Burns free-kick was cleared, but the ball was pumped back into the penalty area, falling for Mike Elwiss, who shot through a crowd of players.

Minutes later Preston were awarded a penalty in what was turning out to be a highly entertaining game. Craggs had pushed Treacy to concede the spot-kick, but Platt saved the penalty, which was taken by the same player.

Two minutes from half-time the home side reduced the arrears when a piledriver from Treacy hit the bar and rebounded to Elwiss, who headed in at the back post.

Preston flew at Boro in the early stages of the second half, but again it was Jack's side which showed how it should be done.

Just six minutes had gone when Bobby Murdoch sent David Mills clear. His cross was headed in by Brine for his second and Boro's fourth.

Preston were determined to go out in a blaze of glory and Platt had to punch clear under severe pressure.

The home side continued to press in the final half hour of the season. There was plenty of goalmouth action, but no more goals.

* * * * *

Triumphant skipper, Stuart Boam, is carried shoulder high by his teammates as they celebrate their promotion after victory over Oxford United.

REFLECTIONS

Alan Foggon

A player who would be on anyone's list of bargain buys, that was Alan Foggon.

Picked up by Stan Anderson for £10,000 from Cardiff City the season before, Foggon fitted into the style Jack Charlton wanted to play like a hand fitting into a glove.

Running deep from midfield, Foggon would latch on to balls expertly delivered from Messrs Armstrong, Murdoch and Souness.

Powerful and difficult to knock off the ball, Foggon often used to barge his way through tackles, coming out with the ball from a seemingly impossible position. And then there was the eye for goal.

Alan scored in Boro's first game, he scored in the last and he scored in 16 others in between, ending the season as leading scorer with 19 goals.

"I was enjoying my football again, " he says freely. "I had won my first trophy when I was a 19 year old with Newcastle, but had gone of the rails a bit.

"I had moved down to Cardiff, but that didn't work out, and when Stan came in for me it was great to be able to move back to the North-east.

"I had never envisaged anything like what happened when I came home, although I don't think we got the recognition we deserved at the time. We were respected, by some people, but that was it. I don't think anyone realised just how good we were at the time, probably including ourselves."

For the players at the time it was just a case of getting on with the job. There was little time for basking in self glory. The team didn't stop to think about its list of achievements, or how and what they were doing. It was almost as if all the success was accepted and dealt with on an every day basis.

A comparable team today would, given the explosion in football coverage, have its stars plastered across bedroom walls the length and breadth of Britain.

Twenty-five years ago there was nowhere near the exposure for the game.

"We enjoyed what we did and Jack wouldn't let anybody get carried away," explains the West Pelton born goalscorer.

"Not that anybody would. There were no big time players there. Jack and Bobby Murdoch had seen and done it all, but there was no superstar feeling about the place at all.

"Jack put together the final pieces of a jigsaw. They completed a team which was started by Stan Anderson and Harold Shepherdson."

The jigsaw fell off the table in one match, as Foggon well remembers.

"We all had our own roles in the team and we trusted each other to get on with it. We played to a certain game plan and it worked, but we were sussed out at Wrexham in the FA Cup.

"It was a filthy day, the pitch was like a bog, the rain lashed down and Wrexham stayed in their own half for long periods. It meant that when I was running on to a long ball, I was running straight into a crowded part of the pitch and we just couldn't get going at all in the conditions.

"Wrexham were in the division below us as well. It's funny that they could stop us, but most of the Second Division couldn't.

"When we were thrashed 5-1 at Forest the week after, I think a few of the fans thought the wheels had come off. They had suffered from false dawns before, but we never lost faith in our own ability and you can see by the results that we came flying back. We drew the next game and won nine after that.

"There were many games which spring to mind, apart from Forest and Wrexham. The 8-0 beating of Sheffield Wednesday, the wins over Oxford and Luton on successive Saturdays which brought us promotion and then the championship, the 4-0 win in Bobby Moore's debut at Fulham. He didn't know what day it was!"

All this followed a stay on Ma Charlton's 'health' farm.

Jack had bought his mother a house at Middleham on Carlton Moor. Players with weight problems, either too much or not enough, were invited to stay for a week, or longer, while they received the 'treatment' deemed necessary.

Foggon was accompanied by reserve team goalkeeper Maurice Gormley and coach Jimmy Greenhalgh, who made sure there was plenty of exercise to go with the special diets.

The idea was to strip at least seven pounds from the 13st frame of Boro's leading scorer, therefore giving him an extra yard of pace. It clearly worked.

"That season as a whole was so special, whatever you were doing, on or off the farm and it was all so simple. Jack didn't re-invent the wheel you know, he just got it to move faster than most that year."

The regrets came after.

"We should have won the league the first year we were up. If the club had bought a couple of new players in certain areas I'm sure we would have won the Championship, or at least made a genuine challenge for it. That's how good we were."

APPROXIMATELY 30,000 fans lined the streets of Middlesbrough to see their heroes parade in an open topped Bee-Line coach on the Sunday after the final game.

Bands were playing as the players waved to the crowds and captain Stuart Boam was presented with a commemorative scroll by the Mayor, Walter Ferrier.

CHAPTER TWELVE
POST SEASON BUSINESS

BORO'S season did not finish with their final league game. They still had an eye on a couple of other matches which needed to be played.

On the Wednesday after the season finished for Boro, Luton, who had gone up in second place, lost 4-3 at home to Sunderland, thus giving Boro a record points winning margin for any senior British league.

Two days later a crowd around 30,000 strong turned up at Brisbane Road to watch Orient take on Aston Villa. Orient needed to win, but drew 1-1, a result which meant that Carlisle were to go up with Boro and Luton and play First Division football for the first time in the club's 70 year history.

Playing at Aldershot on the Wednesday in a testimonial game for centre-half Ricky Walden, a full-strength Boro side lost 1-0 to a Terry Bell headed goal on the stroke of half-time in front of 5,027 fans.

The team was: Platt, Craggs, Spraggon, Souness, Boam, Maddren, Murdoch, Mills, Hickton, Foggon, Armstrong.

On the way home from a benefit match at Tunbridge Wells on the Friday, Boro's players took in the FA Cup Final, watching Liverpool beat Newcastle 3-0.

They returned to Teesside to field a near full strength side for a cricket game on the Sunday when they played a benefit match for Ayresome Park groundsman Wilf Atkinson at Normanby Hall. Boro scored 113-7, John Hickton making 32, but lost by six wickets as a result of Graeme Hedley's unbeaten half century.

It was reported at the time that Boro's coach, Ian MacFarlane, had the batsmen in two minds for most of the game. Whether to be hit for four or six!

Two players missed the game. Jim Platt had gone home to Ireland and Bobby Murdoch was a guest at the Scottish Cup Final watching his former club Glasgow Celtic beat Dundee United 3-0.

Other football news saw Sir Alf Ramsey sacked as manager of the England team after the country failed to qualify for the World Cup Finals in Munich.

His record, however, spoke for itself. In charge for 113 games, Ramsey's England had won 69 games, including the 1966 World Cup Final itself, losing only 17.

"It's a sad day," said Boro's assistant manager Harold Shepherdson.

"He was personal friend of mine all the way through. I admire him and despite what the critics have said I think he will be a sad loss to football."

Sir Alf wasn't a great communicator with the press and many felt this hadn't helped him when the going got tough.

Failure to win promotion also cost Vic Crowe his job as manager of Aston Villa, while Bill Gates hit the jackpot with his testimonial game.

The match, Leeds United, champions of the First Division, against Middlesbrough, champions of the Second, drew a crowd of 31,643 to Ayresome Park.

Only the Boxing Day crowd against Sunderland was bigger that season. Leeds, who had played a 0-0 draw with Sunderland in a repeat of the 1973 FA Cup Final in a testimonial game for Billy Bremner the night before, drew 4-4 with Boro in Gates' big night.

A former Spennymoor schoolboy, Gates had played for 12 years with Boro and made an estimated £16,000 from the game.

Alan Foggon with a hat-trick and David Mills were the scorers for Boro, while Joe Jordan, Terry Yorath, Peter Lorimer and Billy Bremner scored for Leeds.

Boro's next testimonial was just up the road at Newcastle. A crowd of 27,938 turned out to watch the beaten Cup finalists take on the Second Division Champions in a benefit game for Tony Green.

Bobby Charlton played for Newcastle, with Jack at centre-half for Boro. Eight goals were scored in the game, five by Newcastle, with John Tudor scoring a hat-trick to go with goals from Alex Bruce and an own goal from former Newcastle player John Craggs.

Boro's goals were scored by John Hickton, Alan Foggon and Malcolm Smith.

Boro: Platt, Craggs, Spraggon (Cochrane), Souness, Boam, J Charlton (Taylor), Murdoch (Brine), Smith, Hickton, Foggon, Armstrong.

Newcastle: Burleigh, Crossan (Gibb), Kennedy, McDermott, Howard, Moncur, Bruce, Green (Barrowclough), Tudor, Hibbitt, R Charlton.

The Ayresome Park pitch was acknowledged to be one of the best surfaces in the country thanks to the dedicated work of long-serving, and soon to retire, groundsman Wilf Atkinson.

The Redcar and District Amateur Operatic Society were on hand to sing a farewell to Middlesbrough as they set off on an end of season tour to Norway, the Society's current production being A Song Of Norway.

Boro beat Stavanger Vikings 3-1 with goals from Malcolm Smith, Alan Foggon and Stuart Boam all in the first half. They went on to beat Norwegian Second Division leaders Vard by 4-0 with goals from Smith 2, John Hickton and a Jim Platt penalty.

Local bookmakers had Boro as 4-6 favourites to be the top North-east team the following season, with Newcastle at 5-4 and Carlisle 25-1.

The odds for the First Division Championship had Boro at 16-1, Newcastle at 33-1 and Carlisle at 200-1, with a special bet offering 4-5 on the Cumbrians being relegated.

"It's nice to be rated," said Charlton. "So often when you go into the First from the Second, people write you off. The bookies never give anything away and if they think those odds are right I would tend to go along with them and say they are very likely.

"I think they have seen enough of the quality of our play and our players to know we are going up into the First Division to stay there and not just to fight against relegation."

David Mills and Willie Maddren missed the tour of Norway as they were away playing for the England Under-23 team.

Mills was soon to be called into the England squad proper after Stan Bowles, of QPR, walked out after being substituted.

Caretaker manager Joe Mercer said: "There is no place for Stan after that. I have had good reports about David from Under-23 manager Ken Furphy and have no hesitation in bringing him into the side."

Mills was in the squad for games against East Germany, Bulgaria and Yugoslavia.

David Armstrong and Brian Taylor didn't return with the rest of the team from Norway. Instead they joined Boro's junior side for a tournament in Rotterdam, while Jim Platt entered hospital to have his tonsils removed.

Boro were to be invited to play in the following season's Texaco Cup.

The competition was to include all the 1973-74 First Division clubs from England and Scotland who were not involved in a European tournament, plus the first and second teams from the Second Division - Boro and Luton - as well as the champions of the Third and Fourth Divisions, Oldham and Peterborough.

During the closed season Jack Charlton was named as Manager Of The Year, beating off the challenge of Don Revie at Leeds and Bill Shankly at Liverpool, both of whom were to resign that summer. Shankly quit the game, while Revie took over as manager of the England national team.

Charlton was awarded a cheque for £1,000 and two gallon bottles of Bells Scotch Whisky.

Other divisional awards: Division One, Bill Shankly (Liverpool); Division Three, Jimmy Frizzell (Oldham); Division Four, Noel Cantwell (Peterborough).

Charlton was also awarded the OBE in Her Majesty The Queen's Honours List, while he denied reports which suggested he would take over at Villa following the sacking of Vic Crowe, and later at Leeds, as they searched for a successor for Revie.

"I have begun something here and I want to see it through," said Charlton. "I have no intention of going to any other club."

Chief coach Ian MacFarlane left to take over as assistant manager at Manchester City, linking up with his old friend Tony Book.

Jimmy Greenhalgh took over as chief coach until John Coddington arrived from a similar position with Bradford City. Coddington was a centre-half in his playing days with Blackburn and Huddersfield.

Previous boss Stan Anderson resigned as boss of AEK Athens shortly before the end of the season.

These days televised football matches are accepted, even expected and are welcomed by clubs who see them as an extra source of income.

Currently SKY TV pay participating clubs a substantial amount each time they feature on a scheduled Sunday afternoon programme.

But it wasn't always the case. For many years TV companies were less than welcome at grounds, with clubs believing that their prescence had a drastic affect on attendances.

Certainly Boro were none too happy to have them around and chairman Charles Amer was outspoken in his criticism and forthright in his views with regards to what should be done.

"When we put a match on the screen it takes the place of 100 people on the terraces," explained Amer, continuing: "They would pay £45. We get £55 from the TV people, so we make only £10.

"If BBC Radio do second half snippets we get £3.46, if they do second half commentary we get £26. If local radio cover the match we get nothing.

"An 'away' side appearing on Match Of The Day receives only £600."

Amer revealed that in the 1972-73 season, the 92 league clubs received £2,045 each from TV and radio fees and that, he said, simply wasn't good enough.

"We dont want the public, especially those in hospitals and the old folk, to be deprived of their TV football, but we feel we are entitled to a bigger piece of the cake from TV.

"It is the condition of the compensation which concerns us. We want £3.5m for one year between us, not spread over three. If we were to get a bit more from the pools, TV and radio, football clubs would be self supportive. The financial restructuring of football should have taken place years ago."

Amer produced figures to back up his demands, explaining: "The Players' Union receives £25,000 a year, but that should be £125,000.

"On £3.5m a year, spread over 50 matches, it works out that 10,000,000 watching soccer on TV would get it roughly for half a penny a week. I should like the football clubs to get £3.5m a year plus £7.5m out of the football pools. In other words, £60-£70,000 a week from TV, and £150,000 a week from the pools.

"With all things added we would be giving £1,500 a week to Third and Fourth Division teams, £3,000 a week to Second Division teams and £4,000 a week to those in the First Division.

"In return, in addition to snippets used during the week on screen, like Match Of The Day and The Big Match, I feel TV and radio should be allowed to broadcast one match live every weekend, in full.

"Football is entertainment and big business. As well as the skills of the players it involves making money."

Jack with his proud family outside Buckingham Palace after receiving his OBE.

REFLECTIONS

Jim Platt

Jim Platt was handed his first team debut by Stan Anderson in October 1971 and the young 'keeper grabbed it with both hands.

When Jack Charlton arrived at Ayresome Park eighteen months later, Platt was already an ever present in the side. His initial meeting with the new manager, however, caused him some logistical problems.

"At the end of the 72/73 season, " Jim recalls, " I'd gone home to N.Ireland to visit my family. I hadn't been there long when I received a phone call to return to Middlesbrough for a team meeting with the new manager.

"We met Jack at the Marton Hotel in what was a rather low key affair but what he did promise us was that we would all be given a fair chance to stake a claim for a place."

From the outset of his reign Charlton preached that football was basically a simple game and that his new team would play to it's strengths.

He therefore set about developing a style of play which suited the players he'd inherited. But as Platt vividly remembers, gaining the respect and confidence of the team had its early explosive moments.

"It has to be said that Jack was a very fair man but he insisted that we played the game his way or not at all.

"The only time he really lost his rag was after Fulham had beaten us 2-0 in our first home game. He was in a foul mood when we returned to the dressing room. I remember an empty Lowcocks lemonade crate flying through the air as he vented his anger about our inept display and how we'd let the fans down.

"In all honesty he had a point. What he was trying to emphasise was that even if you don't win a game you should make sure that you don't lose it because at the end of the season it's amazing how those drawn games all add up."

The post match dressing room " discussion " worked wonders as the Boro went on an unbeaten league run which lasted into the new year. However, as Jim recalls, having a settled, disciplined, injury free side certainly enhanced their promotion ambitions.

"If you look at the squad it was a bit threadbare in key positions. If we'd lost the likes of John Hickton, Graeme Souness, Willie Maddren or Bobby Murdoch for any length of time it might have been a different story.

"We also had a good disciplinary record. I remember Graeme Souness being sent off at Carlisle for punching Stan Ternant. We were leading 1-0 at the time but by the end of the match we were hanging on for the draw. Jack

had no sympathy for Graeme at all saying he got what he deserved."

Like most of the players from that period Platt highlights the crucial signing of Bobby Murdoch as the pivotal point in the season.

"We were certainly going to have a good season what ever happened, but when Jack bought Bobby he proved to be one hell of an asset. He brought a quality of passing to the team which fitted the system, particularly the cross field diagonal ball to David Armstrong. And although people said his legs had gone when he came to us, he was still a very difficult man to get past. He was really strong and well built."

Over the course of the season Jim Platt won numerous man of the match awards and had a remarkable record of keeping clean sheets in 50% of the matches in which he played. But speaking very modestly about that fine achievement he says,

"To be honest in some of the games I didn't have a great deal to do because we defended so well as a unit. Jack emphasised that we should defend all over the pitch and many of the teams in that division couldn't cope with our constant pressure.

"Occasionally in a tight game I was called upon to make a crucial save and I'd like to think that some of my performances in those games earned us extra points."

For a generation of supporters, the 1973-74 season was undoubtedly the pinnacle of their Ayresome Park memories. And the same can be said for the players. As Platt frankly admits,

"That season was definitely the highlight of my career without a doubt. Even better than playing in the World Cup in Spain. It was the perfect season. A team of great lads all pulling together. A time I will never never forget."

Although it may have been the perfect season, Jim still harbours one significant regret and ruefully confides,

"From a professional point of view I wish I'd played in all the league games. That would have meant a great deal to me. But when it was obvious we were promoted Jack understandably started to chop and change the team to have a look at some of the fringe players and Pat Cuff played in a couple of matches."

Like most of Charlton's promotion winning side the overall highlight was the season itself. But certain games do stick in Jim's memory.

"Our 1-0 win at Luton. The day we won the championship. That was special because they were the eventual runners up. It was a tough game and I had quite a bit to do and was pleased with my own performance.

"Obviously West Brom and Fulham away, the two 4-0s, were great. And doing a lap of honour around Ayresome Park after all the results had gone in our favour the day we beat Oxford 1-0.

"But for me the 8-0 home win against Sheffield Wednesday capped the season off nicely.

"Before that game there was a rumour going around Middlesbrough that if we got a penalty that day I was going to take it because I was the only member of the team who hadn't scored. Although I was a more than useful outfield player, there would have been no way that Jack would have let me take a penalty. In his eyes it would have been unprofessional."

The underlying feeling that emerges from talking to the Boro players, and Jim Platt in particular, is that they all respected Jack Charlton's tactical ability. Even if at times he was prone to lapses of memory when he couldn't remember their names.

But those constant bouts of amnesia only added to the humour and created a positive dressing room atmosphere.

"Jack was a very shrewd manager indeed. The best I've ever come across," enthuses Platt.

"He could make crucial tactical switches at half-time which often affected the course of a game. We all had confidence in his judgement."

Once in the First Division Charlton's Champions were immediately challenging for honours. But the allegation that Jack failed to take them on a stage further is partly refuted by Platt who candidly points out,

"What many people forget is that the Middlesbrough job was Jack's first in management. He was learning all the time. On the whole I feel he was looking for value for money in the transfer market. But in hindsight we all realise now he should have bought either David Cross or Ray Hankin to replace John Hickton.

"However, from a personal point of view, playing for Middlesbrough under Jack Charlton did my international prospects no harm whatsoever."

Although Jim Platt was unfortuate to be around at the same time as the outstanding Irish 'keeper Pat Jennings he went on to win twenty-three caps for his country and like all his teammates he still remembers the season of 1973-74 with great affection.

CHAPTER THIRTEEN
A SEASON OF RECORDS

- Championship won with six matches still to play.

- Promotion won with seven matches still to play.

- Highest ever number of points for a Second Division side (two points for a win) = 65.

- Biggest ever winning points margin - 15 - in the Second Division (two points for a win) beating ten point margin set by Leicester in 1936-37 season.

- British record for winning league (two points for a win) - 15 points - beating 14-point total set by Morton over Clyde in Scottish League Division Two 1963-64 season.

- Longest unbeaten run in the club's history = 24 games. Previous record = 21 games in 1926-27 season when the club lost its opening four games.

- Most doubles in a season = nine.

- Record number of consecutive league wins = nine.

- Equalled club record of just one home defeat in a season.

- Club record over 42 game season of just eight goals conceded at home.

- Club record over 42 game season of most away wins = 11.

- Club record over 42 game season of fewest away defeats = three.

- Club record over 42 game season of fewest goals conceded away = 22.

- Club record over 42 game season of most wins in a season = 27.

- Club record over 42 game season of fewest defeats in a season = four.

- Club record over 42 game season of fewest goals conceded in a season = 30

- A run of 20 home games without defeat.

- Twenty-five clean sheets from 42 games in the league plus two in five games in the cups = 27 from 47 games.

- Jack Charlton named overall Manager Of The Season, having also been awarded Manager Of The Month for September and March.

- Run of six games without conceding a goal plus run of just one conceded in eight matches. Both runs were a record at the time and have only been bettered by the 1987-88 side which had one run of seven without conceding a goal, including a run of just one goal conceded in ten matches.

- Beat previous seasons points total with 11 games still to play.

- Despite all the records and success, the club still reported an overall loss of £2,470 for the season, although the following season they made a profit of £140,000, which was a record profit at the time.

APPEARANCES
Armstrong 42, Boam 42, Maddren 42, Foggon 41, Hickton 40, Platt 40, Craggs 39, Spraggon 39, Mills 38, Souness 34, Murdoch 33, McMordie 7, Smith 6, Brine 5, Taylor 4, Cochrane 3, Creamer 3, Cuff 2, Gates 1, McAndrew 1.

PLAYING SUBS
Smith 11, Brine 6, H Charlton 2, Gates 1, McMordie 1, Mills 1, Murdoch 1, Poskett 1, Souness 1.

GOALS
Foggon 19, Hickton 11, Mills 11, Souness 7, Armstrong 5, Murdoch 5, Boam 4, Smith 4, Craggs 3, Maddren 3, Brine 2, Spraggon 1, Taylor 1, own goal 1.

FA CUP APPEARANCES
Armstrong 2, Boam 2, Craggs 2, Foggon 2, Hickton 2, Maddren 2, Mills 2, Murdoch 2, Platt 2, Souness 2, Spraggon 2.

PLAYING SUBS
Brine 1, Smith 1.

GOALS
Armstrong 1, Mills 1.

LEAGUE CUP APPEARANCES
Armstrong 3, Boam 3, Craggs 3, Foggon 3, Maddren 3, Murdoch 3, Platt 3, Spraggon 3, Hickton 2, Smith 2, Souness 2, Brine 1, Gates 1, Mills 1.

GOALS
Brine 1, Foggon 1, Smith 1.

PLAYING RECORD
P 42 W 27 D 11 L 4 For 77 Against 30.

Every regular outfield player scored during that season.

Average attendance: 22,498, compared with 10,400 the previous season.
National average attendances season 1973-74:
First Division: 28,292
Second Division: 13,693
Third Division: 6,199
Fourth Division: 3,926

1973-74 Final League table

	P	W	D	L	F	A	Pts
MIDDLESBROUGH	**42**	**27**	**11**	**4**	**77**	**30**	**65**
Luton Town	42	19	12	11	64	51	50
Carlisle United	42	20	9	13	61	48	49
Orient	42	15	18	9	55	42	48
Blackpool	42	17	13	12	57	40	47
Sunderland	42	19	9	14	58	44	47
Nottingham Forest	42	15	15	12	57	43	45
West Bromwich Albion	42	14	16	12	48	45	44
Hull City	42	13	17	12	46	47	43
Notts County	42	15	13	14	55	60	43
Bolton Wanderers	42	15	12	15	44	40	42
Millwall	42	14	14	14	51	51	42
Fulham	42	16	10	16	39	43	42
Aston Villa	42	13	15	14	48	45	41
Portsmouth	42	14	12	16	45	62	40
Bristol City	42	14	10	18	47	54	38
Cardiff City	42	10	16	16	49	62	36
Oxford United	42	10	16	16	35	46	36
Sheffield Wednesday	42	12	11	19	51	63	35
Crystal Palace	42	11	12	19	43	56	34
Preston North End*	42	9	14	19	40	62	31
Swindon Town	42	7	11	24	36	72	25

*1pt deducted

CHAPTER FOURTEEN
INTO THE FIRST DIVISION

JACK Charlton may have been tempted to make a couple of close-season signings to help the Boro squad on their return to the First Division for the first time in 20 years.

However, in the event, there were no new faces and the talented team which romped away with the Second Division title was given every opportunity to do itself justice in the top flight.

Clearly the players had every belief in their own ability, while Charlton was certain that his squad was good enough and that the team's commitment and pattern of play would be very effective in the First Division.

Boro's defensive formation would have few problems coping, with Stuart Boam and Willie Maddren as good as any central-defensive pairing around. Behind them, they had a top quality international goalkeeper in Jim Platt.

Midfielder Graeme Souness had improved over the last 12 months to become a much feared and respected player, which had earned him a place in the full Scottish international squad.

Up front, Boro had the triple partnership of David Mills, John Hickton and Alan Foggon, who had ripped defences to shreds in the Second Division.

The fans were full of anticipation. They had flocked back to Ayresome Park in huge numbers during the promotion campaign. Attendances had rocketed by an average of more than 12,000 to over 22,000. As a result, gate receipts were almost trebled from £55,131 in the previous season to £148,298.

Even so, Boro's costs were increasing all the time and, despite not having spent a single penny on incoming transfers, Boro lost £2,470 over the promotion year. Much of the profits had been spent on ground improvements, while Boro were still paying off their World Cup loan, eight years after the event.

There was one major change before the start of the new season. Head groundsman Wilf Atkinson retired after 28 years with the club. Wilf, 66, was respected throughout the country for the excellent condition of the Ayresome Park turf.

Boro could hardly have made a better start to the new campaign. Their first fixture was away to Birmingham City, and there were one or two worries because Boro had to travel to St Andrews without Graeme Souness. Brian Taylor was drafted in to play his first game for the team for almost 12 months. Otherwise Charlton was able to field his first choice line up.

Any fears quickly dissipated. Boro were an absolute revelation. They trounced hapless City by 3-0 with Foggon making an electric start by scoring a brace of goals, and John Hickton netting the other.

Unfortunately Boro were unable to maintain this momentum. A little bit of complacency crept in and a shock home defeat by 2-0 at the hands of fellow promoted Carlisle United was followed by a tame 1-1 draw with Luton Town, who had finished runners up to Boro in the Second Division.

Finally Boro got it together again with a 1-0 midweek win at Carlisle United, thanks to a David Armstrong goal. But it was destined to be only Boro's second win in their first seven games, despite battling draws against Stoke City and Chelsea.

However, normal service was quickly resumed and Boro soon got to grips with the rigours of the First Division. Consecutive wins against Manchester City, Tottenham and Wolves finally set them on their way.

Seventeen years old striker Alan Willey from Houghton le Spring was introduced into the starting line-up against Manchester City, when Hickton was used an an emergency left-back in place of Frank Spraggon. Willey quickly settled in and scored one of the goals in his third match against Wolves.

Charlton was not afraid to pitch in the kids and the next player to make his debut in the First Division was 18 year old striker Bill Woof, who came on as a substitute in a 3-1 home defeat by Queens Park Rangers.

The third debutant before Christmas was another young 18 year old striker. Tommy Paterson from Newcastle played in a 3-0 home win against Birmingham City in December. It was to be his one and only appearance for the club.

The fact that Charlton had been forced to blood three young strikers was an indication that there was a weakness in attack, especially when any of the regular players were injured or suspended. However the manager resisted the temptation to go out and buy the big name striker who might have made all the difference, even though the funds were available.

August 1974: Big Jack holds aloft his Manager of the Year trophy as Boro start their first campaign in the top flight for over twenty years.

Goalscoring had not been a problem in the FA Cup, where Boro marched through to the sixth round thanks to victories against non-league Wycombe Wanderers, after a replay, Sunderland and Peterborough United, again following a replay.

It left Boro with a sixth round tie against Birmingham at St Andrews, where they had triumphed by 3-0 on the first day of the season. Many thousands of Boro fans made the pilgrimage to the Midlands anticipating the club winning a place in the semi-finals of the FA Cup for the first time in their history.

However, the match was to end in disappointment. Boro never functioned as well as they could and went down to a 1-0 defeat to a goal from Bob Hatton on a miserable afternoon. Maybe a top class striker would have made the difference.

Terry Cooper was Jack Charlton's first cash signing.

When Charlton finally took out the cheque book, it was not to sign a forward, but a left-back. Boro paid Leeds United £50,000 for the former England star Terry Cooper, who was now 30. Cooper was top quality and added a lot of experience to the Boro back four, but he was to be the only cash signing made by Charlton in the first two years of his reign.

Boro finished the 1974-75 season with two consecutive wins against Liverpool and Coventry and ended in seventh place in the First Division. It was a marvellous achievement and fully justified the manager's belief that the team was good enough to hold its own in the top flight.

This was the highest league position by any Boro side since 1950-51, when they had finished sixth with a squad which included legendary names like Wilf Mannion, George Hardwick, Alex McCrae, Harry Bell, Johnny Spuhler and Rolando Ugolini.

The fans roared back to see Charlton's team in the First Division and the average attendance soared to a magnificent 28,605 in the first season back in the top flight. It was an increase of more than 6,000 on the previous season.

The result was a mammoth record profit for the club of £140,000, which allowed them to comfortably wipe out every penny of their previous deficit of £80,000.

The extra cash came mainly through the turnstiles, which at £229,000 was £83,000 up on the previous year. Season ticket sales had zoomed, doubling to £146,000, while £88,000 came from cup revenue and £63,000 from the shop and development association.

Unfortunately seventh position was to be a feat which Charlton was unable to repeat during the final two years of his time at the helm at Ayresome Park, even though there was clearly cash available to try to bring in the big money buys which might have made all the difference.

Boro remained a highly competitive and efficient First Division side, but they slipped to 13th position the following season and improved only slightly to 12th in Charlton's final campaign.

The only trophy which Boro achieved during Charlton's three years with the club in the First Division was an inauspicious one, the Anglo Scottish Trophy. Boro beat Second Division Fulham by 1-0 on aggregate in the two legged final.

However Boro did go very close to glory in the Football League Cup, when they stormed through to the semi-finals in the 1975-76 season to qualify for a two-legged clash with Manchester City. They overcame Bury, Derby County, Peterborough United and Burnley, all at the first attempt, to reach the last four.

Boro entertained City in the first leg at Ayresome Park and won 1-0 thanks to a goal from John Hickton. But they were held up in traffic on the way to the second leg and were forced to change on the coach. This far from ideal preparation left its mark, because City quickly scored two

Phil Boersma failed to make an impact at Ayresome Park.

Charlton announced his resignation in the summer of 1977. It was not unexpected, for Jack had always maintained that he would stay no longer at Ayresome Park than four years.

However, his departure was still a disappointment for many fans, because Charlton had achieved so much in taking the club from the Second Division and establishing them as one of the best in the land. At the same time, the club's playing fortunes had more or less stood still for the past two years.

But Charlton's contribution on Teesside should never be underestimated. He gave the town back its self respect after 20 years in the doldrums and set up a level of expectation among the fans which still lingers today.

His ability to organise his team and get the very best out of players has not been bettered by any manager since. On the down side, fans look back at Charlton as a manager who was not keen to spend the club's money.

If nothing else, Jack will be remembered by fans everywhere for that one tremendous season in the Second Division when Boro swept all before them. The division has arguably never seen a more accomplished all-round side. It was the season that fans' dreams are made of and it will remain in the record books for ever.

goals to take the lead on aggregate and before going on to win 4-0 on the night.

Charlton's only foray into the transfer market that season was to sign Liverpool's utility forward Phil Boersma, for £70,000. The player arrived on Teesside with a good First Division pedigree and plenty of experience, but did not make the anticipated impact.

The hard work which was being put into Boro's youth scheme was beginning to pay big dividends and Scottish teenager Tony McAndrew broke through into the side towards the end of the campaign. The following season he established himself as a first team regular.

The 1976-77 campaign was Charlton's last on Teesside. The team was still strong and organised, and capable of winning something. But they still lacked a top quality striker.

Charlton attempted to fill the breach by bringing in the former Hull City and Millwall forward Alf Wood, who was now in the latter days of his career. Wood, who had just celebrated his 31st birthday, was a good professional, and had enjoyed an excellent league career. But he was not the answer at Ayresome Park and, although he was popular with both his teammates and the fans, Wood scored just two goals in 23 league appearances.

REFLECTIONS

Jack Charlton

JACK Charlton had spent 22 years with one of the most successful club sides in English Football.

But his time with Leeds United was coming to an end and management was the chosen path for the 37 year old centre-half.

"These things are chosen for you, you don't choose them yourself," he says firmly.

"I had been left in no doubt that my days were numbered and that management was a good idea.

"In my final season I was sharing first team duties with Gordon McQueen. I would play in the more important matches as we brought him along.

"I had passed my coaching badge ten years beforehand and I felt I could do a job."

"I had played at a very high level for many years and I was happy to pack the playing side in. Preparing for this or that high profile game every week had taken its toll. I had just got sick of it.

"I could probably have played into my Forties but when your enthusiasm starts to go it's time to pack it in. I would have played for Boro if there had been any injuries, but we didn't have any."

Dr Neil Phillips was the doctor for both the England team and Middlesbrough at the time and it was he who approached Charlton asking if he would like to take the Middlesbrough job.

"I knew that I didn't want to run a pub or a shop and that management was a way of staying in the game. I watched Boro a couple of times, realised they were quite useful and saw there was something to work on. There was distinct promise in Stan Anderson's team."

The first thing Charlton had to do was to get to know his team.

"I was at a dinner with Jock Stein soon after I had taken over. He asked me what I had lined up as far as pre-season friendlies were concerned.

"I told him 'nothing', as I had just taken over. He told me to leave it to him. He would organise accommodation, training facilities and a couple of matches in Scotland for us.

"He said I should live with my players for a week to ten days, and that way I would get to know them far more quickly. He was dead right. I learned more in that tour of Scotland than I would have done in two years under normal circumstances.

"We played Morton, Hamilton and Partick and I sorted out who I could work with and who I couldn't, the good from the bad.

"You will always find those who will try and sort out everybody else's problems at the same time as causing trouble themselves. Bloody barrack room lawyers.

"You have to get to know your players off the field, and their characters, if you are to get the best out of them.

"Get rid of the ones you can't work with. I wouldn't have any cliques in my dressing room. There would never be any players who preferred to sit next to one another. I wanted to make sure that when my players got on the bus, they weren't bothered who they sat next to."

Everyone has their own idea of how and why his first venture into management worked. The man himself explains the theory behind the success with Middlesbrough that season.

"The catalyst was Alan Foggon. He had won the England 220 yards championship as a schoolboy and he could shift a bit.

"The game in England was going nowhere and I saw an opportunity to play a different game. But we needed pace to exploit it. To adopt a system to beat the one being played.

"I had watched too many matches in the previous couple of years which had ended in stalemate, with players ten yards either side of the half-way line playing offside.

"We played it simply. John Hickton would peel away, David Mills, the front man, would run towards the ball, and Alan Foggon would run deep from midfield, with David Armstrong a secondary midfield runner.

"The mistake was to give Alan the ball at his feet. He was fast, but give him the ball to feet and he would fall over it, scrape his face and we'd all have a good laugh!

"But play it properly and he was devastating.

"We had great passers of the ball, like Armstrong and Souness, when we straightened him out, and from September Bobby Murdoch. We exploited a situation in the game at that time."

Charlton's philosophy was straightforward - keep it simple.

"If you try to change the structure of the team you won't achieve it by giving them something different to do every Saturday, nor if you ask different players to do different things.

"Give players too much to think about and they will forget everything you told them within five minutes.

"This was proved when we went to Lilleshall for a training session.

"There was a doctor who we were told was going to give us a lecture. Well you can imagine what a lot of footballers thought about that.

"But he rammed home the benefits of simplicity. He told us to pick two teams. He gave each player a word to remember before they played in a game. At half-time none of the players could remember the word.

"He told the same players the same word again and at full-time only two of the 22 could remember. That was one of the most valuable lessons I ever learned."

Where Jack Charlton had set his stall out with a routine and set of disciplines which stayed with him, brother Bobby was taking over at Preston in the same division.

"I thought Bobby had made a wrong choice," he says openly. "I thought he could do better for himself than Preston. They weren't a good side, whereas the one I had taken over was.

"It was a shame the way it worked out for him, but there was little chance of anything else happening because they weren't much good to start with."

Jack moulded a winning side with a lot of hard work and encouragement, with just one addition, Bobby Murdoch, and achieved something which will surely never be bettered, or even matched.

"Bobby was the capture of the season. Maybe of any season. He was the best passer of the ball in the business and the only reason Jock Stein gave him to me was because Tommy Burns was coming through at the time and Bobby might not play all the games with Celtic because of his age.

"You would swear blind that when he passed the ball to Alan Foggon it would speed up to catch him or slow down to wait for him!"

It is inconceiveable that a manager could turn a half decent team into such a formidable record breaking force by making just one signing in a season. But that is exactly what he did.

"I knew we would win the league at Christmas. It was then the penny dropped with the players with regard to what we wanted them to do.

"I didn't re-invent the game. Nothing has changed in football since I was a kid, not on the field anyway. Off it it has changed tremendously. I used to handle all the player negotiations, it was me who did all the work to get Bobby Murdoch here.

"I spent a lot of time with the Celtic manager Jock Stein when I started out and it was through him that Bobby came to us. Jock was a master, he helped me so much and I learned a hell of a lot from him.

"These days all financial matters are taken care of elsewhere within the club. But I was always hands-on in that department."

It was the lack of activity which, in the eyes of many, cost Boro further glory.

"They're right," reflects Jack. "If I hadn't been so tight with the money we could have had another couple of players which might have made all the difference in our first year up."

"It wasn't so important the first year, because we were head and shoulders above the rest. But we should have done better that first year in the First Division.

"It wasn't all my fault. I told the lads that in any game if we were winning and the clock showed time, not to even think about scoring another goal. Just to get the ball into the corner and keep it there. That way everyone was back behind it and the opposition would have to come through the entire team to get it.

"There was one big game at Derby where we won a corner. Bobby Murdoch should have played it back to the man who took it, but he sent it into the middle. I was up off the bench screaming at him, but we won another corner.

"This time he played it on to someone who played it to someone else who passed it to Boamy. He helped it on to Willie, who had no chance of getting it clear. They scored in the last minute and went on to win the league.

"I was looking forward to playing in Europe. I knew Europe well, having played so often there with Leeds. We missed a good chance that season. We only missed out by a couple of points."

The criticism comes from a man who had a go at his own team when they won the Second Division Championship!

"We went to Luton needing two points to win the league, but I thought it would be better if we only took one, then won the Championship at home to Notts County a week later.

"I told the lads they did not need to win the game. I was on the touchline yelling at them to let Luton score. But would they hell. I have never tried to fix a game, you understand, but I thought we would get more glory and more accolade if we won the league at home. It's always better to win championships at home.

"Millsy scored and we won 1-0. I know the players were delighted and so was I. It was a great achievement, but I had a go at them afterwards, as much as you can when you've won the league."

It was Charlton who helped Mills overcome a slight crisis of confidence early into his reign.

"Players will always pick on one player in the dressing room. That player is the one who bites and rises to the bait. David rose every time.

"I took him in the office, sat him down and we had a few words. I told him to smile and agree with them and that if he didn't bite, the lads would soon get pretty sick and pick on someone else. He didn't and they did.

"If I hadn't acted when I did and he had carried on, he could have become a recluse. But look at him now, he's doing television and radio and he is a confident man.

"A few of the lads would have a go at me and I didn't mind, but they knew how far to go. I remember when the comedian Freddie Starr came to our training ground to take part in a television documentary of some sort.

"John Craggs flattened me with a tackle and I chased

him right around the pitch.....as the cameras kept rolling!"

"But Willie Maddren was the biggest mickey taker out of me."

Despite all the success achieved in his first year, Charlton still says that his biggest regret in football lay with Middlesbrough.

"A friend of mine, who I respected, Jim Bullock, formed a players union. We used to talk a lot and he always said that you should never stay anywhere longer than four years.

"After that, he said, players had heard it all and you wouldn't be able to motivate them the same way. I left Boro after four years. I know now that I left early. I should have stayed another year.

"But nothing will ever take away the memories I have of my time at Ayresome. Among all the time I have been in the game, my experiences there were some of the best I have known. They weren't all good, but they were an experience.

"I am quite pleased that what I have done in the game of football I have done my way, which is maybe not the way other people have done it. I'm a good coach, I know what I want and how to get the best out of people."

There were times when Charlton used to let his temper get the better of him. It was at such times that he was grateful for the guidance of Harold Shepherdson.

"Shep used to say to me 'Don't go into the office in that mood, just wait a few minutes and calm down'. He was right, of course.

"Shep was great for me, a real stabiliser. He used to go and watch all the opposition for us, knowing the way we played the game. He knew what to look for and ways we could hurt the opposition.

"My coaching staff was good, too. Ian MacFarlane was my right hand man during that season, but he left at the end of it and he changed.

"I bumped into him a couple of years after at Carlisle. He was smartly dressed and I commented on his jacket. "'What do you care?' was his response. So, I thought, right, if that's the way you want it.

"Jimmy Greenhalgh was as good as gold but he had no control over the players. He wanted to be friends with them all and couldn't control them all that well as a result. But he was very good at his job.

"I have always believed in management that players should know how far to go.

"I told Jimmy Headrige that I wanted to know everything that was going on. Some people think that managers don't need to know everything but I wanted to know the lot and often he would come up and say I think you should have a word with such and such a player, or this and that player needs sorting out. That way everything was nipped in the bud because I knew what was going on."

There were arguments of course, as Charlton outlines:

"I had ructions with the secretary, Harry Green.

"Harry was a Charlie Amer man. I had arguments with Charlie about many things, but never football. He never once interfered with the playing side of things.

"As for Harry, well secretaries are often the type who think they know where all the secrets are hidden. I was always taught that secretaries were there to take care of the administration and nothing else. He became too involved in team affairs.

"I attended only two board meetings all the time I was there. I don't know how I would get on these days with spending millions and having to deal with a financial director.

"But managing Middlesbrough that season was easy. The difficult job I had was at Sheffield Wednesday where I had no money to spend, a team which was bottom of the table, with players who weren't much good and where the supposed good ones turned out to be anything but.

"It took us a year to sort that side out, to realise all you need to get out of the Third Division is a big goalkeeper, a big centre-half and a big forward.

"With Boro, I had a good team and I came out smiling."

At the end of the 1973-74 season everyone did.

Charlton's Champions: Thanks for the great memories.

Autographs